Software Design with COBOL & SQL

COMPUTER STUDIES SERIES

Consulting Editor

DAVID HATTER
BSc (Eng), CEng, MCBS, MIMechE
Department of Systems and Computing Studies
Polytechnic of East London

This is the first series to present an integrated approach to the complete range of topics needed by students of computer studies who are currently on Higher National Certificate and Diploma courses, or the first two years of a degree course. While each book is designed to stand alone, together they provide a comprehensive view of computing, with emphasis given to its applications in business and industry.

THE COMPUTER STUDIES SERIES

Software Design with COBOL & SQL

Piers Casimir-Mrowczynski
Series Editor: David Hatter

Blackwell Scientific Publications
OXFORD LONDON EDINBURGH
BOSTON MELBOURNE

Blackwell Scientific Publications
Editorial offices:
Osney Mead, Oxford OX2 0EL
25 John Street, London WC1N 2BL
23 Ainslie Place, Edinburgh EH3 6AJ
3 Cambridge Center, Suite 208
  Cambridge, Massachusetts 02142, USA
107 Barry Street, Carlton
  Victoria 3053, Australia

First published 1990

Set by DP Photosetting, Aylesbury, Bucks
Printed and bound in Great Britain by
Billing & Sons Ltd, Worcester

DISTRIBUTORS
Marston Book Services Ltd
PO Box 87
Oxford OX2 0DT
(*Orders*: Tel: 0865 791155
       Fax: 0865 791927
       Telex: 837515)

USA
Publishers' Business Services
PO Box 447
Brookline Village
Massachusetts 02147
(*Orders*: Tel: (617) 524-7678)

Canada
Oxford University Press
70 Wynford Drive
Don Mills
Ontario M3C 1J9
(*Orders*: Tel: (416) 441-2941)

Australia
Blackwell Scientific Publications
(Australia) Pty Ltd
107 Barry Street
Carlton, Victoria 3053
(*Orders*: Tel: (03) 347-0300)

British Library
Cataloguing in Publication Data
Casimir-Mrowczynski, Piers
  Software design with COBOL & SQL.
  1. Computer systems. Programming
  languages: COBOL language
  I. Title
  005.133

  ISBN 0–632–02604–9

Library of Congress
Cataloging in Publication Data
Casimir-Mrowczynski, Piers.
    Software design with COBOL & SQL/
    Piers Casimir-Mrowczynski.
      p.   cm.
    ISBN 0–632–02604–9
      1. COBOL (Computer program
  language)   2. SQL (Computer program
  language)   3. Computer software—
  Development.   I. Title.
  II. Title: Software design with COBOL
  and SQL.
  QA76.73.C25C3724   1990
  005.13′3—dc20   90-30068
                                       CIP

Contents

Preface   vii
Acknowledgements   ix
Introduction   x

Part 1 – The techniques

1 Program specifications   3

2 Program design   10

3 Formalised data structured programming   23

4 Program characteristics   46

5 Programming standards   55

6 Program testing   60

7 Structured walkthroughs   68

8 Program maintenance   72

9 Documentation   75

10 Charting techniques   82

Part 2 – Practical examples

11 The development of a batch COBOL/SQL system   99

12 The development of a screen based SQL system   123

13 A SQL report   136

14   A COBOL/SQL car insurance and quotation system   142

Summary   152

Index   157

Preface

COBOL (Common Business Oriented Language) was originally developed over 20 years ago, back in 1959. Since that time it has been continually reviewed, changed and enhanced. Its popularity has increased many-fold, with common acceptance as the business language for all standard business applications. Now a widely accepted and widely used medium it is still evolving, not only in its implementation but the way in which it is used.

Now also available is SQL (Standard Query Language). SQL takes COBOL into the next phase of its life and addresses the problem of using new database technologies with the proven flexibility of COBOL. SQL is discussed, with examples, later in the book.

At a technical level COBOL, although a standard language, actually has many derivations. Different manufacturers have created their own versions, some with additions to the standards and others with omissions. The changing face of computer technology has also influenced the language. With the development of viable and usable database systems and interactive systems new facilities have been introduced with new methods established to handle such changes. No longer are the majority of programs written to run overnight overseen by an operator. These new technologies demand new approaches, verbs, ways of testing and so on. Although such obvious changes do have an effect, the more subtle programming nuances also need to be addressed.

With changes in COBOL there have followed major changes in the use of the language and the business situation it is used in. The role of the programmer has changed and he or she must learn to adapt. It is for these reasons that I decided to write this book. No longer do we want or need more books that describe how to write 'bubble-sorts' in COBOL or demonstrate the workings of punch card machines. No longer are COBOL programmers bearded gurus or computer 'whizz kids'. Industry now needs, and hopefully demands, dedicated professional programmers who know how to 'deliver' a quality product in a professional business environment.

Like many of my potential readers, I learnt COBOL the hard way, using punched cards and paper tape to write programs that bore no relation to the business world whatsoever. Now, being involved in recruiting and training COBOL and SQL programmers to fit our corporate computing philosophy

I still detect the lack of formal training that addresses the wider programming issues. Seven levels of nested 'IF'S' might look pretty but they do not impress me or the poor maintenance programmer assigned to untangling them!

We now want thinking programmers. Programmers who believe in simple but concise code, who include comments within their programs, who work to standards, communicate with their managers and perform well in a team. Formalization does not have to mean regimented and boring. It means success, respect, meeting deadlines, user regard, promotion, bonuses and money and so it goes on. That is what industry now demands.

However, what industry wants and actually receives are not always the same. There still remains the catch 22 situation of 'no experience, no job – no job, no experience'. This book is, therefore, aimed specifically at those learning COBOL and perhaps SQL for the first time in a place of education, without direct work experience, and those who are just starting in the industry. What the book will also do is reaffirm the COBOL concepts already taught, as well as addressing the broader issues of programming in an organised computing department.

Glance at the 'Contents' listing. How many of the terms can you claim to have had fully described to you. Programming standards? – 'We never did those on our course'. Yet more and more Data Processing (DP) departments or Management Information Services (MIS) are using them and expect them to be used. Working on a project? What does working on a project or in a team really mean and what is Time Management?

COBOL and SQL have an important role to play but it is now not sufficient to know the languages. They have to be applied within the wider concepts of the professional business world which means understanding the business, knowing the language and how to apply it in a structured and well organised way. It also means being part of a department that believes in such philosophies with far-sighted managers, team leaders and programmers who will adopt and promote such ideas. If such methodologies are not being used then use one of the programmer's most important skills; communication. Suggest a structured approach, demonstrate the advantages and sell the idea. Do not always wait for others to come to you, go to them. Your ideas will not always be accepted but they could sow the seed!

So what next? Read the book. Use Part 1 to increase your knowledge and let it act as a reference. Keep the book near your desk or wherever you may be working. Although there is no such thing as a stupid question, this book should answer many of them. Let the second section help develop you into the kind of accomplished programmer industry demands. Try to apply, where appropriate, what you see. Consider the broader issues, form your own opinions and turn them into success. Success at interviews, success in your first job and success all the way through your career!

Finally, a brief message, 'COBOL is an industry language and is not the property of any one company or group of companies, or of any organisation or group of organisations'.

Acknowledgements

In producing this book I would like to the thank the following: Terry Gould, Kevin Honey and Paul FitzGerald, the best managers anyone could ever wish for, who all guided and encouraged me in their own ways. Eric Coates for guiding me towards a successful education in computing and Julian Sellen for always encouraging my writing. Finally but by no means least, much gratitude to Jeremy Swinfen-Green who liked my idea and gave me the opportunity of publishing it, Robin Arnfield, Commissioning Editor, and David Hatter for his guidance.

I would like to thank David Hatter, David Leigh and Roy Newton for their permission to use material on Structure Clashes from their book, *Software: design, implementation & support*, published by Paradigm.

Introduction

COBOL was first developed over 20 years ago. Since that time it has been extensively used, mainly in a commercial environment. There exist literally millions of lines of COBOL code in the world today, reflecting a massive commitment in terms of both time and money – no one is going to throw that investment away without thinking very carefully first.

Before we look any further at the need for COBOL, it is perhaps worth asking the question – Why use COBOL anyway? The simplest answer is probably that COBOL has become an industry standard. When it was first introduced only a comparatively small number of computer languages existed. This was because of the way computers and their associated software evolved, most of the then existent languages were scientifically oriented. Those scientific languages were designed to handle accurate calculations but were weak in the area of text handling and the structuring of large amounts of data. Commercial organisations relied heavily on manual labour and adding machines, often in the shape of rows of desks with many clerical staff. Nowadays the role has very much reversed with far fewer clerical staff and arguably higher skill levels required.

As computers grew in power and decreased in size, becoming less science oriented, their general worth became more widely recognised. COBOL slowly developed and became available, generating a greater computer 'audience'.

COBOL, when introduced, was one of the first attempts to address a different and new user. The newly computer-wise commercial sites recognised the power of COBOL in a business context. COBOL was established as the business language. Large systems were written and many new programmers became conversant in the language. Commercial packages could now be written by organisations, confident in the knowledge that many COBOL sites existed that could buy and maintain such software. Soon it became too dangerous and uneconomic to standardise on any other language. COBOL programmers began to proliferate and became generally available in an expanding market.

There now exist thousands of programs written in COBOL. The cost of rewriting systems is huge, both in terms of overall effort and time. Remember, time really is money. It is for these reasons that COBOL is widely used and accepted as the industry standard. Other languages do of course exist and commercial systems are written in them. Some of the more popular have included BASIC, RPG and FORTRAN. The commercial market place is still dominated by COBOL and it continues to hold its place. With the ability to embed SQL into COBOL programs, COBOL has a new lease of life.

COBOL has now changed significantly since its first early versions. New verbs have been added whilst others have been taken away. Individual manufacturers have added their own facilities to take advantage of new hardware or environments. The recent proliferation of microcomputers in business has meant the introduction of micro oriented versions – these can provide features to facilitate screen handling, peripheral control etc., on a limited memory machine.

In the mainframe world, perhaps the most significant changes have been the interfacing of various database structures and COBOL. Traditionally, COBOL has held and assessed data files organised either sequentially or indexed sequentially. With the wider use of database structure facilities have been included to access data organised in this way. Specific database navigation–retrieval statements can be embedded into COBOL statements, for example SQL. Data can then be retrieved from or added to the database and of course manipulated in the usual COBOL fashion. Three database organisations are commonly used; network, hierarchical and relational. Relational databases are currently proving the most popular with a number of large manufacturers providing specific support and new database handling tools. Database structures will be more fully explained later in this book.

The second largest change is the growing number of on-line or transaction processing systems – systems designed to be used interactively, often coupled with database systems, that allow instant access to data. Screen handling software has meant new verbs to handle such demand. Effective and complex applications can now be built, still using COBOL, to service such needs. Although enhancements to the language have been necessary the basics still remain the same.

With the widespread introduction of database structures available to COBOL users, software designers are now looking at other ways in which they can enhance the total COBOL environment. As such interactive applications take over from batch-only systems so have new tools been created to assist in their development. Screen painters are now becoming common. These allow the analyst/programmer to 'paint' an enquiry/update screen on-line, introduce validation procedures and generate the necessary code to complete the job. Such tasks can be carried out more quickly than would be possible using only traditional COBOL. Further tools to support general systems design, documentation and maintenance are also being marketed.

With such developments continuing, even the COBOL critics must admit that the future of the language is secured for a number of years to come. Although not true to its original form, the language continues to maintain its standard core, thus allowing COBOL programmers to maintain and enhance what are very marketable yet transportable skills.

Perhaps the reason for COBOL's long life is its ability to change with the needs of commerce. It is still a growing language, able to provide the facilities and structures demanded today. If it continues to adapt then its need will remain for as long as businesses continue to use computers.

PART 1

The techniques

Part 1 describes the stages and methods involved in actually creating usable software. It considers the way programs written in COBOL are designed, written and maintained. Practical examples are included to illustrate the approaches used.

Even before a program is written, much effort will have been put into its inception. There has to be a need for the program in the first place. This will be the result of a feasibility study, analysis and design of an overall system. Only then will program specifications be written. Of course, the system could already have been in place for some time. In that case, program specifications would be provided as part of an on-going systems maintenance plan.

From the specification the program design begins using a recognised design technique. By this stage a lot of effort has been applied without a single line of code being written. Only then does programming begin.

Part 1 describes the stages from program specification, design, programming standards to testing and maintenance. All require a methodical approach if a usable, working program is to result.

CHAPTER 1

Program specifications

The end result of the analysis phase will be a series of program specifications. Program specifications come in many guises – some are written to such a detailed level that they almost represent a completed program while others are written at very much a business function level. The ideal is likely to lie somewhere between the two. Too much detail and the process of program writing becomes a tedious coder's chore; too little detail and the program is only going to be completed after much asking of questions and is likely to contain many inaccuracies.

Program specifications will always vary depending on the application involved i.e., an on-line screen program specification is going to vary from that of a large batch validation program or report program specification. Again, if the program is to be written for a database application, the specification will also vary.

Writing specifications is no simple task. Time needs to be spent to create a complete and well structured document that is easily understood and lacking in ambiguity. This raises two important issues of specification writing; structure and content. If the structure is good but the content lacking then the document is of little use. In addition, if the content is sound but the structure confused then much time will be spent trying to order and collate the information given.

A very simple example program specification follows. Its purpose is to describe the basic structure recommended for a simple 'extract of data program'. Remember that the specific application type will, to some extent, dictate the final form.

An example program specification

PROGRAM SPECIFICATION.

EXCT01.

ABC MANUFACTURING PLC.

Contents

(1) Contents
(2) Introduction
(3) System flowchart
(4) Input
(5) Output
(6) Processing
(7) Appendix

Introduction

EXCT01 forms part of the customer mailing system. It is an extract program.

The program reads the customer name/address file and extracts records matching any combination of five possible criteria. Matched records are written to an extract file for processing by the label printing program PRCT01.

The program will be run every two months as a batch job using supplied parameters.

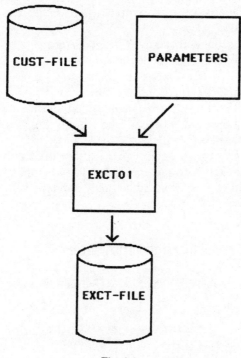

Fig. 1.1

System flowchart

See Fig. 1.1.

Input

The following file is used:

```
CUST-FILE.


01   CUST-REC.
     03   CUST-NAME              PIC X(25).
     03   CUST-ADDR.
          05   ADDR-LINE1        PIC X(25).
          05   ADDR-LINE2        PIC X(25).
          05   ADDR-LINE3        PIC X(25).
          05   ADDR-LINE4        PIC X(25).
     03   CUST-AN-CODES.
          05   CUST-ANALYSIS1    PIC X(02).
          05   CUST-ANALYSIS2    PIC X(02).
          05   CUST-ANALYSIS3    PIC X(02).
          05   CUST-ANALYSIS4    PIC X(02).
          05   CUST-ANALYSIS5    PIC X(02).
     03   CUST-BAL-CF            PIC S9(5)V99.
     03   CUST-BAL-BF            PIC S9(5)V99.
     03   CUST-CREDIT            PIC S9(4)V99.
     03   CUST-RATING            PIC 9.
     03   CUST-CONTACT           PIC X(25).
```

Parameters are in the format: XXXXXXXXXX

Output

The extract file should be in the format:

```
EXCT-FILE


01   EXCT-REC.
     03   CUST-NAME              PIC X(25).
     03   CUST-ADDR.
          05   ADDR-LINE1        PIC X(25).
          05   ADDR-LINE2        PIC X(25).
          05   ADDR-LINE3        PIC X(25).
          05   ADDR-LINE4        PIC X(25).
```


Processing

The aim of EXCT01 is to create an extract file using data gathered from the customer mailing system. One record is generated per customer selected.

Initialisation

Open files, obtain the five possible parameters. Check that the parameters are valid codes – if not report and terminate the program.

Main

Read the customer file sequentially. When any of the parameters matches any of the customer analysis codes, create an extract record in the output format described.
  Continue until end of file.

Termination

Close all files and stop run.

Appendix

Valid analysis codes are:

```
AB
BD
DC
GD
OC
NC
PR
ST
TT
WS
WX
ZZ
```

The resultant program structure could look like this:

```
IDENTIFICATION DIVISION.

ENVIRONMENT DIVISION.

DATA DIVISION.

    CUST-FILE.

01  CUST-REC.
    03   CUST-NAME              PIC X(25).
    03   CUST-ADDR.
         05   ADDR-LINE1        PIC X(25).
         05   ADDR-LINE2        PIC X(25).
         05   ADDR-LINE3        PIC X(25).
         05   ADDR-LINE4        PIC X(25).
    03   CUST-AN-CODES.
         05   CUST-ANALYSIS1    PIC X(02).
         05   CUST-ANALYSIS2    PIC X(02).
```

```
          05  CUST-ANALYSIS3      PIC X(02).
          05  CUST-ANALYSIS4      PIC X(02).
          05  CUST-ANALYSIS5      PIC X(02).
      03  CUST-BAL-CF             PIC S9(5)V99.
      03  CUST-BAL-BF             PIC S9(5)V99.
      03  CUST-CREDIT             PIC S9(4)V99.
      03  CUST-RATING             PIC 9(01).
      03  CUST-CONTACT            PIC X(25).


EXCT-FILE

01  EXCT-REC.
      03  EX-CUST-NAME            PIC X(25).
      03  EX-CUST-ADDR.
          05  EX-ADDR-LINE1       PIC X(25).
          05  EX-ADDR-LINE2       PIC X(25).
          05  EX-ADDR-LINE3       PIC X(25).
          05  EX-ADDR-LINE4       PIC X(25).

WORKING-STORAGE SECTION.

01  WS-EOF                        PIC X(01)  VALUE SPACE.


PROCEDURE DIVISION.
AA-CONTROL SECTION.
A00-ENTRY.
    PERFORM BA-INIT.
    PERFORM BB-MAIN.
    PERFORM BC-TERM.
    STOP RUN
AA99-EXIT.
    EXIT.




****************************************************
*            I N I T I A L I S A T I O N           *
****************************************************
 BA-INIT SECTION.
 BA00-ENTRY.
    OPEN INPUT  CUST-FILE.
    OPEN OUTPUT EXCT-FILE.

    PERFORM ZA-READ-CUST-REC.
    IF WS-EOF = "Y"
        ........

    ACCEPT WS-PARAMETERS.
        ..........

    IF WS-PARAM1 NOT VALID-PARAMETER
          OR
       WS-PARAM2 NOT VALID-PARAMETER
          OR ........

 BA99-EXIT.
    EXIT.
```

```
***************************************************
*             M A I N                             *
***************************************************
 BB-MAIN SECTION.
 BB00-ENTRY.

     PERFORM CBA-DETAIL UNTIL WS-EOF = "Y".

 BB99-EXIT.
     EXIT.



***************************************************
*           T E R M I N A T I O N                 *
***************************************************
 BC-TERM SECTION.
 BC00-ENTRY.
     CLOSE CUST-FILE.
     CLOSE EXCT-FILE.
 BC99-EXIT.
     EXIT.



***************************************************
*      E X T R A C T   D E T A I L S              *
***************************************************
 CBA-DETAIL SECTION.
 CBA00-ENTRY.

*   REQUIRED RECORD?

     IF WS-PARAM1 = CUST-ANALYSIS1 OR
        WS-PARAM2 = CUST-ANALYSIS2 OR
        WS-PARAM3 = CUST-ANALYSIS3 OR
        WS-PARAM4 = CUST-ANALYSIS4 OR
        WS-PARAM5 = CUST-ANALYSIS5
        NEXT SENTENCE
     ELSE
        PERFORM ZA-READ-CUST-REC
        GO TO CBA99-EXIT.

*   RECORD IS REQUIRED,SO CREATE EXTRACT RECORD.

     MOVE CUST-NAME TO EX-CUST-NAME.
     MOVE CUST-ADDR TO EX-CUST-ADDR.

     WRITE EXCT-REC.

*   READ NEXT RECORD FOR PROCESSING.

     PERFORM ZA-READ-CUST-REC.

 CBA99-EXIT.
     EXIT.


 ZA-READ-CUST-REC SECTION.
 ZA00-ENTRY.
```

```
READ CUST-FILE
    AT END
    MOVE "Y" TO WS-EOF.

ZA99-EXIT.
    EXIT.
```

Although this example is quite straightforward, consider how easy it is to create a program from the details given. File layouts can be slotted into the framework and the processing broken down into sections and also added.

Later examples deal more specifically with actual program design.

When writing specifications yourself be clear in the structure you adopt but also give thought to the general content – this is most likely to apply to the 'processing' section. Try to consider the person who will be working from your specification and the way he or she should structure their code. Ask yourself a number of questions. Is there ambiguity? Is complex processing adequately described? Are assumptions made? Are file layouts etc., consistent with any other programs in the suite?

Remember, writing a bad program specification is easy, writing a good one is a demanding task but also a worthwhile investment in time.

Exercise

Program specifications

(1) Write down four advantages in being provided with a program specification.

(2) Outline the structure of a program specification that you would consider suitable to specify a screen based enquiry program.

How does it differ from the batch-processing based example given above?

CHAPTER 2
Program design

Program design is an important part of programming – get it wrong and much time will be wasted, resulting in project slippage, a poor final result, inefficient processing and an unsatisfactory view of the programmer who wrote it – get it right and everyone should be happy. When you start as a trainee or junior programmer, the task of program design can seem daunting and perhaps a little haphazard. With a little thought however, the task will be under control.

There is no magical answer to the perfect program design. The program might be a large report generator written to run in batch mode. Alternatively the program could be an on-line enquiry program to be run many times through the day. Whatever the need, by careful program design and following a few simple guidelines, the process will be much simplified and the end result far superior.

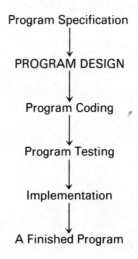

The notion of flowcharts was one of the first design methods introduced. Flowcharts were a charting method whereby the flow of the program was represented by connected boxes. Decisions were handled by diamond shaped boxes with one entry and two exits – one representing true, the other false.

Although flowcharts superficially came across as a new and exciting concept they proved of little value in designing large and complex programs. Indeed they added little value, tending to produce long, thin trails of boxes simply representing the existing code. Programmers would sometimes draw the flowchart afterwards, rendering the exercise almost useless. If flowcharts have any use, it is in their ability to show the handling of small but complex conditions – today they are rarely used.

Using a top-down approach gives:

(1) A consistent approach.
(2) Module empathy.
(3) A structured approach.
(4) A structure that maps onto COBOL constructs.

So how do we set about designing our program? Numerous techniques exist. All take different approaches. Some look at the function of the program, others are influenced by inputs and output to the program whilst others again are driven by the data being processed. If a program is to reflect a flow then every program is going to have a similar structure. By assuming a top-down approach and reflecting this general flow of information, a natural series of steps can be defined.

In designing our program we will first consider the idea of logic design.

Logic design

Logic design is one of the first steps in actual program design. Ideally you will be involved at every stage. It can occur however that different people are responsible for different parts of the program writing.

Logic design itself considers two basic factors, the first being the data being processed and the second, the application under consideration.

The data

In writing any program, consideration needs to be given to the actual data being processed. This is going to fall into two areas; input and output.

The output will be strongly influenced by the program's objective, whether it be to produce a report or update a file via an input screen. The input data will be decided by the application in terms of actual values and to some extent structure. What is even more important is the organisation of the input data.

At some stage of system design there is a good chance that at least one level of data analysis has been performed. This will have looked at the individual data items and is also likely to have considered the final physical organisation of the data. Ideally, the results of such an exercise will be documented in actual file layouts, a technical specification or data dictionary. Data dictionaries are a method used to organise data describing data in a database. Such information can be held on computer, cross-referenced etc.

Use such sources of data to clarify in your own mind the actual organisation of data used. At this stage it is now worth just briefly considering what data analysis involves.

Data analysis basically considers data, its structure, form and use. By performing such a task, the data should imply a particular way in which it can be accessed from a computer systems' point of view. Nowadays numerous data organisations exist. These range from the traditional file structures of data items grouped into records and being accessed sequentially or via an index, through to the true database organisations. Current database structures include hierarchical, network and relational types. Relational databases are discussed later.

The relevance of data analysis to you the programmer is the idea that the data available and the way in which it is organised will have a major influence on the way in which your program is designed and written. In days gone by, all files were organised sequentially – file updates were performed in batch mode by comparing a file of updates against a permanent or master file. The result was a third new file, duly updated. With the introduction of indexed files it is possible to amend, delete and insert all on the same file. With the introduction of database structures new programming techniques now have to be learnt.

The structure of raw business data has always been complex. It is only now that the structure can be truly represented in a computer-based form. Consider the inputs and outputs to your program, the way in which data required is organised. Is the sequence important? Is there much cross referencing? How should error conditions be handled? Consider the technique of one section per file i.e., the reading or writing of a particular file is handled by a single input–output section.

There are no hard and fast rules regarding data and its influence on program design. However, by asking a few simple questions the task will be better handled.

(1) Consider input and output data.
(2) What is the organisation of the data?
(3) Allow for all error conditions.
(4) Where there is a file there is a loop!

Logic design and application

Logic design considers the data and the application being serviced. Any solution produced should reflect the problem being resolved and of course the program specification. The objective of logic design is to produce a clear and straightforward solution. Whilst it will always be the boast of the more experienced programmer that he can code in fewer lines using 'smart' programming, do not be tempted. Such programs whilst economic on code are generally difficult to understand and difficult to maintain.

The use of box diagrams is the easiest method recommended for documenting your logic design and to some extent the idea of logic design and box diagrams must be considered in parallel. By considering the data being processed and its structure, the application and the flow of data, it is possible to design a basic program outline.

Box diagrams are a simple method of using boxes and lines to represent a series of functional operations. COBOL allows itself to be structured using Sections to represent distinct areas of processing. Each Section can be described by a box.

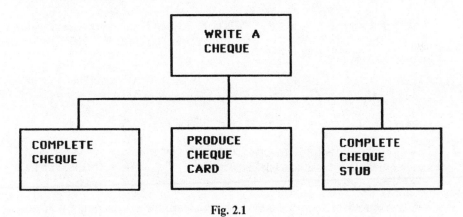

Fig. 2.1

Figure 2.1 describes, in simple terms, the processes involved in writing a cheque using a box diagram. A hierarchical structure is formed that could be further broken down or refined as required. Using this top-down approach functions can be initially defined and then further decomposed.

When designing, consider the data involved first. What is the structure of the data and how is it to be processed. Consider the general data flow using a top-down approach. Obtain a 'piece' of data before you decide how it is going to be processed.

It is generally recognised that there are three basic control structure types – these are; the Selection, the Case and the Repeat Until.

The Selection can be mapped onto the IF THEN ELSE in COBOL. So considering a condition, program flow can be directed in one of two directions. Case performs an action depending on the value of a data item. It is not quite as easy to reflect Case in COBOL, however using a combination of IF statements and 88 levels it is quite possible. Finally the REPEAT UNTIL concept can be applied using IF statements and input–output decisions such as AT END of file.

Selection

```
IF WS-TAX-TYPE = "S"
    MOVE 0.25 TO WS-TAX-RATE
ELSE
    MOVE 0.40 TO WS-TAX-RATE.
```

Case

```
IF WS-OPTION = 1
    PERFORM CA-OPTION-UPDATE.
IF WS-OPTION = 2
    PERFORM CB-OPTION-INSERT.
IF WS-OPTION = 3
    PERFORM CC-OPTION-DELETE.
```

Note   The COBOL structure IF–THEN–ELSE–IF ... could have been used. For the sake of simplicity the more elementary but less efficient IF statement was applied.

Repeat Until

```
PERFORM CB-CALCULATE-BONUS UNTIL WS-EOF = "N".
```

These 'control structures' in terms of logic design relate directly to the data being handled. It is possible to define a number of standard rules that can be applied when processing data.

(1) Always perform an initial READ on the main file. (A technique known as 'read-ahead'.)
(2) After processing a record, read the next one.
(3) Test for positive conditions.

At this stage you will have a basic idea of how the data will be controlled and processed, its structure and type. Now consideration should be given to the actual program design and layout. The suggested method is to use Box and Line diagrams – these are considered next.

Box and line diagrams

When designing any program we must consider many factors. Is the design simple to understand? Has maintenance and enhancement been considered? Is the logical design sound? Box and line diagrams take a top-down approach in an attempt to address these issues. The basic objective is to define individual functions of the program which can then be decomposed either at box-line level or at the next stage of program creation i.e. designing the code.

Box and line diagrams should be designed with the thought in mind that at certain levels a box and its subordinates will map onto a COBOL program section. Other boxes may map onto a piece of pseudo code or directly onto a COBOL paragraph.

Pseudo code is a technique developed to loosely code the structure of a program without being constrained by its specific syntax rules. A simple example of pseudo code might be the following:

```
Print report headings.

Read Record

WHILE NOT eof DO
    Calculate VAT
    Print Invoice
    Read Record
END DO

Print Grand Totals.
```

The above example is extremely simple. It follows no particular language syntax but allows a general processing structure to be written quickly and clearly. Complete program structures can be designed in this way with actual coding following once the design has been suitably refined.

When creating the box diagram consider the functions of the program in a program context. Begin with a box at top-centre containing the program name. Next define three boxes labelled INITIALISATION, MAIN and TERMINATION going left to right.

Remember that flow should always be defined left-to-right. At this stage you should have drawn four boxes without needing to consider the program function to any level of detail.

Now consider the lower functions of the program, with the logic design in mind i.e. the reading ahead principle. What you are doing is creating a simple hierarchy of modules, each with its own specific function.

As a simple example consider the following program specification.

'Write a program to produce money outstanding letters for all customers. The only input is the customer file; output is printed customer letters.
    Report all errors. The program should be called CUSTLT'.

By considering the principles of logic design we can immediately identify an opportunity for 'read ahead' processing. The main driving file is the customer file which is also the only input. The objective of the program and the only output is to produce printed customer letters for customers with outstanding balances.

Our basic box and line diagram will begin by looking like Fig. 2.2. This can now be further refined to include the boxes shown in Fig. 2.3.

This is of course a very simple diagram. It does however act as an excellent piece of documentation. It would be a simple matter to explain the function of the program you were writing just from this picture. As programs become more complicated such diagrams become much more useful. It also becomes

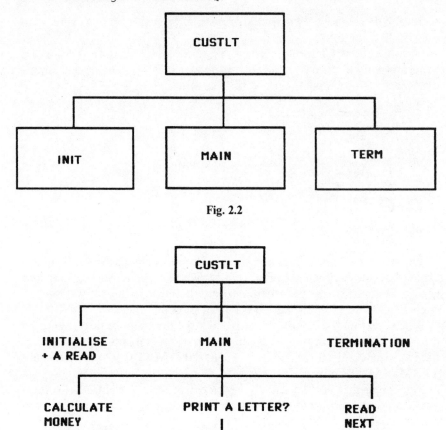

Fig. 2.2

Fig. 2.3

useful when checking your design for consistency, completeness and viability.

In creating a logical design you are well on the way to coding your program. So far we have considered logical designs and box and line structure diagrams. To arrive at the point where you are ready to begin coding consider the following steps.

(1) Consider input and output data.
(2) Always perform an initial READ on the main file.
(3) After processing a record, read the next one of the main file.
(4) Design a box and line diagram with COBOL in mind.

One final stage worth investing a little time in is that of design review. Spend a few minutes reviewing what you have produced. Is the design broken down into enough levels? Are there ambiguities or duplication of module function? Do design and program specification tally. Spend a few minutes checking!

At this stage you should now be in a position to actually code your program.

Physical program design

At this level you should have a good idea of the layout of your program. There will, of course, be an overall Control section subdivided into the three lower Initialisation, Main and Termination sections.

Map major boxes of your diagram onto appropriately named program sections. Naming conventions should reflect the general hierarchy of your diagram.

The program structure, when defined, should be outlined in the Identification Division along with the program name. Include comments to describe the function of the program, modification boxes etc.

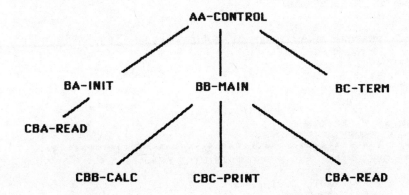

Note CBA-READ is included twice in the structure although it would only be coded once. Perhaps the section could be defined as a subroutine section, using a prefix of Z, for example, ZA-READ.

Sensible SECTION names must be used to compliment the structuring conventions. Prefixes and numbers should be used in conjunction with descriptive names, to describe the section and paragraph names. Order by ascending alphanumerics. At this stage you can define the basic program outline, even if some sections contain no actual code.

```
PROCEDURE DIVISION.
AA-CONTROL SECTION.
A00-ENTRY.
     PERFORM BA-INIT.
     PERFORM BB-MAIN.
     PERFORM BC-TERM.
AA99-EXIT.
     EXIT.
```

with lower sections being included.

The design process is not of course finished. Lower levels of your diagram need to be added although it should now be apparent what Sections are to be included. Each Section should be headed by comments detailing the function of the Section.

Again, it is easy to show the overall structure that will result.

See how the use of PERFORMs reduced the use of GOTOs to an acceptable level.

```
PROCEDURE DIVISION.
AA-CONTROL SECTION.
A00-ENTRY.
     PERFORM BA-INIT.
     PERFORM BB-MAIN UNTIL WS-EOF = "Y".
     PERFORM BC-TERM.
AA99-EXIT.
     EXIT.



 BA-INIT SECTION.
 BA00-ENTRY.
*******************************************************
*** OPEN FILES AND PERFORM INITIAL READ.

     OPEN INPUT  CUST-FILE.
     OPEN OUTPUT PRT-LET-FILE.
     PERFORM CBA-READ.
 BA99-EXIT.
     EXIT.



 BB-MAIN SECTION.
 BB00-ENTRY.
*******************************************************
*** PERFORM MAIN PROCESSING SECTION.

     PERFORM CBB-CALC.
     PERFORM CBC-PRINT.
     PERFORM CBA-READ.
 BB99-EXIT.
     EXIT.
```

```
 BC-TERM SECTION.
 BC00-ENTRY.
************************************************
*** CLOSE FILES AND STOP RUN.

     CLOSE CUST-FILE.
     CLOSE PRT-LET-FILE.
     STOP RUN.
 BC99-EXIT.
     EXIT.
 CBA-READ SECTION.
 CBA00-ENTRY.
************************************************
*** READ CUSTOMER FILE RECORD.

     READ CUST-FILE
        AT END
        MOVE "Y" TO WS-EOF.
 CBA99-EXIT.
     EXIT.


 CBB-CALC SECTION.
 CBB00-ENTRY.
************************************************
*** IS THERE A LETTER TO PRINT?

     IF CUST-BALANCE > 0
           MOVE CUST-NAME TO        PRT-NAME
           MOVE CUST-ADDRESS-1 TO   PRT-ADDRESS-1
           MOVE CUST-ADDRESS-2 TO   PRT-ADDRESS-2
           MOVE CUST-ADDRESS-3 TO   PRT-ADDRESS-3
           MOVE CUST-ADDRESS-4 TO   PRT-ADDRESS-4
           MOVE CUST-BALANCE TO     PRT-BALANCE
     ELSE
           MOVE SPACES TO PRT-RECORD.
 CBB99-EXIT.
     EXIT.


 CBC-PRINT SECTION.
 CBC00-ENTRY.
************************************************
*** IF A LETTER EXISTS, PRINT IT.

     IF PRT-RECORD = SPACES
        GO TO CBC99-EXIT.

     MOVE PRT-NAME TO PRT-RECORD.
     WRITE PRT-RECORD AFTER ADVANCING PAGE.
     MOVE PRT-ADDRESS-1 TO PRT-RECORD.
     WRITE PRT-RECORD AFTER ADVANCING 2.
     MOVE PRT-ADDRESS-2 TO PRT-RECORD.
     WRITE PRT-RECORD AFTER ADVANCING 1.
     MOVE PRT-ADDRESS-3 TO PRT-RECORD.
     WRITE PRT-RECORD AFTER ADVANCING 1.
     MOVE PRT-ADDRESS-4 TO PRT-RECORD.
     WRITE PRT-RECORD AFTER ADVANCING 1.
     MOVE PRT-BALANCE TO PRT-RECORD.
     WRITE PRT-RECORD AFTER ADVANCING 18.

     MOVE SPACES TO PRT-RECORD.
 CBC99-EXIT.
     EXIT.
```

So far we have only really considered the main Procedure Division. As mentioned, the Identification Division can be completed with program name, comments etc. The general structure of the Environment Division can be included next. From the program specification it should be apparent which files are required for input and output.

Detail the Environment Division including all files required, then go on to describe the basic outline of the Data Division. For every file described in the Environment Division include an entry in the Data Division detailing the file descriptions for each file. Conclude this part of the build by adding a Working-Storage Section heading.

```
        IDENTIFICATION DIVISION.
        PROGRAM-ID. CUSTLT.
    *
        ENVIRONMENT DIVISION.
        CONFIGURATION SECTION.
        INPUT-OUTPUT SECTION.
        FILE-CONTROL.
            SELECT CUST-FILE        ASSIGN DISK.
            SELECT PRT-LET-FILE     ASSIGN LP1.
    *
        DATA DIVISION.
        FILE SECTION.
        FD  CUST-FILE
            LABEL RECORDS STANDARD.
        01  CUST-RECORD.
            03 CUST-NAME            PIC X(35).
            03 CUST-ADDRESS-1       PIC X(35).
            03 CUST-ADDRESS-2       PIC X(35).
            03 CUST-ADDRESS-3       PIC X(35).
            03 CUST-ADDRESS-4       PIC X(35).
            03 CUST-BALANCE         PIC S9(05)V99.
            03 CUST-LIMIT           PIC S9(05)V99.

        FD  PRT-LET-FILE
            LABEL RECORDS OMITTED.
        01  PRT-RECORD              PIC X(80)

        WORKING-STORAGE SECTION.

        01  WS-EOF                  PIC X(01) VALUE SPACES.
```

Pseudocode can be useful when coding programs i.e. mapping a block of pseudocode to a particular box. Experience tends to dictate how you use such techniques. Remember that there is always expertise within a department to call upon. If a problem becomes too tricky be prepared to call on others for help – in time, as you learn from experience, it will be your turn to help others.

As you complete more of the program remember to add to your Working-Storage Section. Try to group like items together to form some sense of affinity amongst data items. As you code bear in mind the programming standards your company or department employs. Example programming standards are discussed elsewhere in this book.

To summarise what you should have done so far in completing your physical design:

(1) Create an overall Control structure.
(2) Map higher level boxes onto sections.
(3) Detail the Identification and Environment Divisions.
(4) Write the Data Division and begin the outline Working-Storage Section.
(5) Write the main areas of code as suggested by the lower level boxes.

All the time you should be giving thought to the overall function of the program, programming standards, comments and functional consistency.

Eventually you will end up with a complete program – this is a good time to review the code.

Reviewing your code will take different forms depending on the stage you are at. Initially you should of course review your own code, indeed it could be argued that this is an on-going process. Enlisting the aid of a colleague is a good idea – ask him or her to spend a few minutes looking over your program checking for any 'obvious' mistakes you may have missed and reviewing the general 'look' of the program. Be prepared to return the favour.

Program design is no easy task, it takes practice with the benefit that experience gives. By following the guidelines given, maybe refining them to suit your own style, you are going to be at an immediate advantage over a colleague who approaches the task in a haphazard and unstructured way. You will be be setting yourself milestones which with experience you will be able to measure and estimate both in terms of time and effort.

Summary

The data

(1) Consider input and output data.
(2) What is the organisation of the data?
(3) Allow for all error conditions.
(4) Where there is a file there is a loop!

The logical design

(1) Always perform an initial READ on the main file.
(2) After processing a record, read the next one.
(3) Test for positive conditions.
(4) Consider input and output data.

The program

(1) Always perform an initial READ on the main file.
(2) After processing a record, read the next one of the main file.
(3) Design a box and line diagram with COBOL in mind.
(4) Create an overall Control structure.
(5) Map higher level boxes onto sections.
(6) Detail the Identification and Environment Divisions.
(7) Write the Data Division and begin the outline Working-Storage Section.
(8) Write the main areas of code as suggested by the lower level boxes.

Exercise

Program design

(1) Name four advantages of using a top-down program design approach.

(2) Draw a box diagram describing the production of customer statements for a mail order catalogue.

(3) Refine the above box diagram to define the structure of a workable COBOL program.

CHAPTER 3

Formalised data structured programming

The method of structured programming described in this chapter differs from the previous examples. Previously we have considered program design from a problem solving angle i.e. we have considered the problem and the logic required to resolve it. In this method we take a different approach, we reach a solution by examining the data to be processed and not by the function of the program itself.

This idea was pioneered by Michael Jackson some twenty years ago. There was a realisation that as commercial application became larger and more prolific, a more structured program design methodology was required. The industry was maturing. Slowly people were realising that long and cumbersome flowcharts resulting in even more cumbersome programs would not be the solution. A more radical approach was required and structured methods were devised.

Some of the reasons for such methods were; rising development costs, tighter timescales, greater quality requirements, a need for formal methods and standardisation. This method is just one possible solution.

The basics

Most programs in the hands of a programmer start as a program specification and end as a fully tested and implemented piece of code. The programmer's task is to fill the 'bit in the middle'!

The data structure approach combines the following steps to achieve that goal.

(1) Identify the data involved.
(2) Define the data structures.
(3) Create the program structure around these.
(4) Define the program functions.
(5) Pseudo-code and code.

It is worth briefly describing each phase in turn before identifying the relevant detail of the data analysis and design process.

'Identifying the data' involved is very much that. In the case of traditional

Fig. 3.1

systems identify all the files used and any other input and output data. When addressing database systems, identify the tables or data sets to be processed as well as any additional data sources. Once identified, all the data should be documented in some form. Traditional file layouts are a good start, see Fig. 3.1.

'Define the data structures' concerns the way in which the data relationships are defined, the nature of input and outputs etc. Again the structures need to be physically documented once defined. The use of one of the many charting techniques is a valuable tool to use – annotate accordingly.

Figure 3.2 shows a simple data structure which describes how one teacher has a responsibility for evaluating a number of pupils.

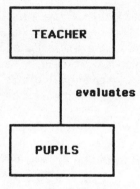

Fig. 3.2

'Create the program structure around these' means that related as well as unrelated data items are used to create the basic program outline or structure. This structure will be embellished to reflect the overall functionality required. Use the available control structures to develop a model that reflects the actual structure of the identified data i.e. if a file has header records and many detail records, this should be reflected in the overall structure diagram produced. Later examples will describe how this can be done.

```
Do While pupils exist
    Evaluate pupil
    Create report
Enddo
```

'Define the program functions' refers back to the program specification. This should be examined and broken down so that all the required operations can be identified and placed within the already defined overall program structure. This is one of the traditional program design stages, i.e. look at the actions that need to be performed and design the program to perform them.

'Pseudo-code and code' is just that. Using the derived structure it is now possible to actually code the final result. What follows is comparatively simple, coding to standards, testing and implementation!

These five steps encompass the data structure approach. Of course, it is not quite that simple but the basic actions remain the same.

The data structures

As we have already seen there are four basic control structures. In this method however, only three are used – the argument being that any structure can be defined from combinations. The Case structure is excluded.

The three structures are:

(1) Sequence
(2) Selection
(3) Iteration

Remember that as we describe each control structure it is being used in a data context. This will become apparent from the worked examples.

Sequence

Sequence describes a number of components or items that always appear in the same series.

In Fig. 3.3 'A' is the Sequence, while '1' and '2' are elements of that Sequence. The Sequence 'A' could be '1','2','3','4' and so on.

In the example shown in Fig 3.4 the Sequence of 'PAY SLIP' would always be made up of a 'GROSS' amount and a 'NET' amount, in other words, a decomposition of the higher level 'PAY SLIP' box.

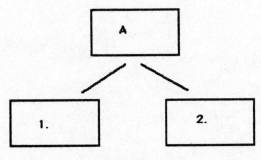

Fig. 3.3

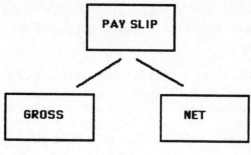

Fig. 3.4

Note that the structure of a Sequence is always shown as a Sequence box with component off-shoots.

```
PERFORM CALCULATE-GROSS.
MOVE GROSS TO WS-PAYSLIP-GROSS.

PERFORM CALCULATE-NET.
MOVE NET TO WS-PAYSLIP-NET.
```

Selection

Selection describes something from which only one item can be selected. In Fig. 3.5 'A' is a Selection of '1' or '2'.

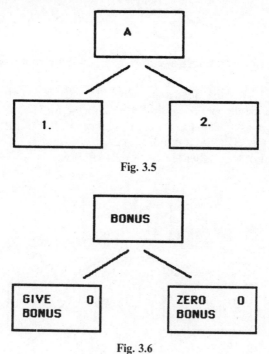

Fig. 3.5

Fig. 3.6

In Fig. 3.6 the bonus given can either be a bonus or a zero bonus, it cannot be both.

Note the use of an 'o' on the structure diagram. This denotes a Selection option and is a standard symbol.

```
IF CREDITS > 15
    PERFORM CALCULATE-BONUS
    ADD WS-BONUS TO WS-GROSS
ELSE
    MOVE ZERO TO WS-BONUS.
```

Iteration

An iteration is an entity which contains zero or more duplicate items. In entity modelling terms this appears very similar to a one-to-many relationship. Such ideas and terms are expanded in Chapter 10.

On a structure diagram an iteration is shown in Fig. 3.7.

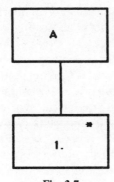

Fig. 3.7

Note the use of an asterisk in the second box. This shows the component that can be duplicated i.e. making up zero, one or more iterations.

So, the used car showroom consists of a number of used cars as shown in Fig. 3.8.

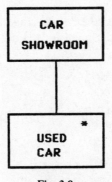

Fig. 3.8

```
PERFORM PRINT-CAR-DETAILS UNTIL END-OF-CARS.
```

These three basic control structures, Sequence, Selection and Iteration, form the basis for creating data structured program designs.

(1) Sequence
(2) Selection = o
(3) Iteration = *

These three structure indicators should not be mixed on the same box diagram level.

The type of control structure used at any particular time will certainly be influenced by the data identified but, just as importantly, by the way in which it needs to be processed. When you write programs you probably use data files or database tables and data sets that you have used previously in other programs. However, you are not necessarily processing those files in the same way, you could be using them very differently.

Consider a customer address file. On one occasion you might be accessing it randomly to confirm a customer address interactively. Another time you could be doing a mailshot across all customer addresses. The processes, although equally valid, are different.

Structure diagrams will vary depending on what data is being processed, how it is being handled and who is looking at it.

Before going on to consider a practical example, let us first examine one or two of the other data structure design idiosyncrasies.

The control structures play an important part in the interpretation of any structure diagram. You must be very precise in their use. Always 'desk check' your diagram against the original requirements. It should be possible to read back the diagram and construct the nature of the data. Again, remember to use the notation correctly, it plays a major part in diagram interpretation. Finally, remember that any method is only as good as its inputs and utilisation – 'garbage in, garbage out'.

A practical example

The example below describes some of the stages involved in program design using the data structure design method. As a reminder, the five stages are performed as follows:

(1) Identify the data involved.
(2) Define the data structures.
(3) Create the program structure around these.
(4) Define the program functions.
(5) Pseudo-code.
(6) Code.

Our example describes a simple customer order system.

This is the input data.

CUSTOMER FILE.

HEADER RECORD.	RECORD COUNT.	PIC 9(5).
	LAST MAILSHOT.	PIC 9(6).
CUSTOMER RECORD.	CUST. NO	PIC 9(7).
	CUST. NAME	PIC X(25).
	CUST. ADDRESS	PIC X(100).
TRAILER RECORD.	RECORD COUNT.	PIC 9(5).

The customer file has one header record, many customer records and one trailer record.

The output data is shown in Fig. 3.9.

CUSTOMER REPORT LAYOUT.

```
                          CUSTOMER   REPORT
DD-MMM-YY                 ----------------        PAGE 9999

CUST NO.                  CUST.  NAME/ADDRESS
--------                  -------------------

99999     XXXXXXXXXXXXXXXXXXXXXXXXX
          XXXXXXXXXXXXXXXXXXXXXXXXXXXXXXXXXXXXXXXXXXXXX

99999     XXXXXXXXXXXXXXXXXXXXXXXXX
          XXXXXXXXXXXXXXXXXXXXXXXXXXXXXXXXXXXXXXXXXXXXX

99999     XXXXXXXXXXXXXXXXXXXXXXXXX
          XXXXXXXXXXXXXXXXXXXXXXXXXXXXXXXXXXXXXXXXXXXXX

99999     XXXXXXXXXXXXXXXXXXXXXXXXX
          XXXXXXXXXXXXXXXXXXXXXXXXXXXXXXXXXXXXXXXXXXXXX

99999     XXXXXXXXXXXXXXXXXXXXXXXXX
          XXXXXXXXXXXXXXXXXXXXXXXXXXXXXXXXXXXXXXXXXXXXX
```

END OF REPORT

Fig. 3.9

We have described an indexed sequential file layout; records accessible randomly by a key field, and a report layout. For those not familiar with the concept of file header and trailer records, they are simply a means of building in file integrity checks. Such records are also used on occasions to hold overall file information, e.g. the next record number to use. There is one header and trailer in the file.

Main program processing

The main processing is quite simple. First read the customer file header record. If the last mailshot date was over four months ago compared with the current date then update the date and continue, otherwise end.

Process all customer records printing the details for each, as described in the print layout above.

When the trailer record is encountered check that the header and trailer record counts match, if not then report this as an error. Report any errors encountered. End processing.

From the above you should understand what this simple program request is required to do. Of course, in a true data processing environment you should be able to expect such a request in a more standardised form – this may not always be the case however!

Let us now consider how the structured data approach can be applied to the example.

Identifying the data involved

Identifying the data involved is easy. There are two sets of data involved that can be thought of as a primary group and a secondary group. The primary group represents the input data i.e. the customer file. The secondary data group is represented by the output required i.e. the customer report layout. The primary group very much influences what we can and cannot achieve! Other data not falling into either the primary or secondary group would include things such as today's date.

Once identified, the facts should be documented, annotated and used to form part of the documentation. This needs to be a major overhead in time and forms a vital part of the process. Nevertheless the amount of work involved at this stage will obviously be influenced by the type of request.

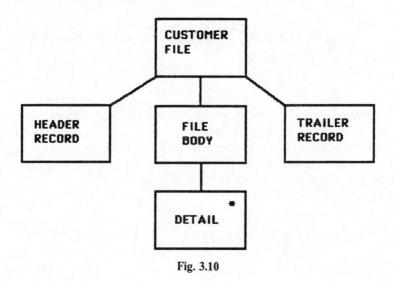

Fig. 3.10

Defining the data structures

Defining the data structures is very much governed by the two sets of data, input and output. The output data is our ultimate goal while the input data is the means to achieve it.

Considering the input data first and applying the control structures we can produce Fig. 3.10.

Note that the detail record is shown as an iteration i.e., there can be zero, one or more customer records. Zero or one records is possible but very unlikely in this example. With zero customers your employer is hardly likely to be be able to afford your services. With the knowledge gained in this book you should be able to get a job anywhere!

Correspondingly, their output data structure can be mapped as in Fig. 3.11.

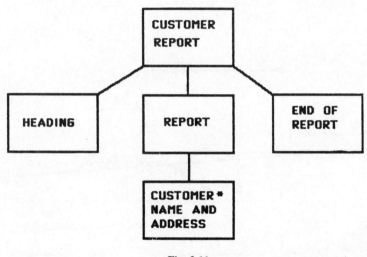

Fig. 3.11

A comparison of the two structures shows that they both consider the data in conjunction with the output required – there exists a strong relationship between the two.

The next stage in the data structure definition process is to 'define the correspondences'. Defining correspondences is an important part of the data structured approach. The correspondences to be defined will exist between input and output data. At this stage much of the data has already been handled so the next stage is reasonably simple.

The two rules commonly used are:

(a) There should be an equal numbers of appearances for each data item.
(b) These data items should be able to be handled at the same time.

Regarding our simple example of input and output structure diagrams and applying the two 'correspondence' rules:

```
CUSTOMER FILE      maps to   CUSTOMER REPORT.

HEADER RECORD      maps to   HEADING.

FILE BODY          maps to   REPORT.

DETAIL             maps to   CUSTOMER NAME &
                             ADDRESS.

TRAILER RECORD     maps to   END OF REPORT.
```

A correspondence diagram is shown in Fig. 3.12.

There are three data items in the input group; Header, Detail and Trailer. There are also corresponding occurrences for these items in the output group under the guises of; 'Heading', 'Customer name and address' and 'End of Report'. So rule (a) holds true.

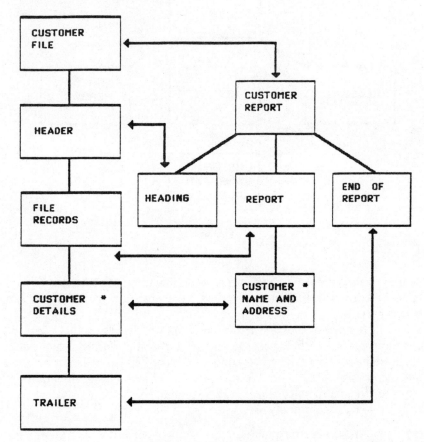

Fig. 3.12 Correspondence diagram

The handling of the data items at the same time is our next concern. With reference to the main processing, the inputs and outputs each data item is handled at the same time. The header record is read and updated immediately. As in good programming practice, if no errors were encountered, we would print report headings – if the report failed then the headings would provide its identity.

For each detail record detail lines are written.

When the trailer record is hit and no errors are found, the end of report line is written. This shows that the report is completed as is a sign of report completeness. If no report trailer were present then it could be assumed that pages were missing.

Rule (b) also appears to hold true.

Programmers often place the input and output structure diagrams together and literally draw lines between correspondences as an integrity check. On more complex structures this can be a very useful check.

Assuming that all is complete then this data structure definition stage is complete.

Creating the actual program structure

Creating the actual program structure is the next stage. Again a set of rules can be applied. This actually makes the process straightforward and again introduces a degree of standardisation into the development process. This is useful in an environment where a number of programmers are all working on a project. Sooner or later someone will have to pick up a colleague's work – following standard procedures eases the hand-over.

The three rules actually act as guidelines on how to approach the program design. The three rules are:

(a) Create a program segment for each 'correspondence' in the data structure.
(b) Include a segment for all processed input 'non-corresponding' items.
(c) Include a segment for all processed output 'non-corresponding' items.

Applying each of these three rules in turn allows us to build up a program structure. As we do so, keep in the back of your mind the way in which the result will be mapped onto a COBOL program – our goal.

Our example provides a simple solution. Take rule (a) first which creates a program segment for each 'correspondence' in the data structure. There are three main correspondences between input and output data groups. This gives us the program structure shown in Fig. 3.13.

After applying rule (a) we should produce a recognisable structure. Notice also that we have included 'segment' names.

Applying rule (b) has no effect in this case as all input items had a correspondence.

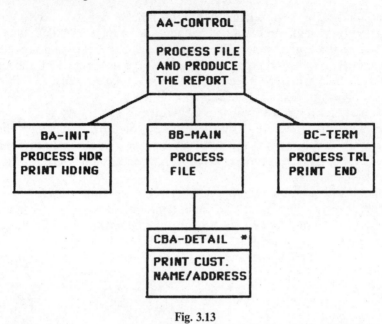

Fig. 3.13

Applying rule (c) has no effect in this case as all output items had a correspondence.

At this stage the overall program structure is complete.

Defining the program functions

Defining the program functions is the fourth of the five stages required to apply the formalised data structured approach. Not surprisingly this builds on the already identified program segments and adds the detail necessary to build a working program.

The functions tend to fall into a few basic categories including: Start, Input, Output, Calculate, Stop. The object of function definition is to match specific processes against defined structure segments – but, working within defined rules.

By studying the structure arrived at above and considering the basic operational categories we can begin to design the program logic. Using a table is one suggested method:

```
NO.     OPERATION.                              CATEGORY.
---     ----------                              ---------
 1.     BEGIN                                   START
 2.     OPEN CUST FILE                          INPUT
 3.     OPEN PRINT FILE                         INPUT
 4.     READ CUST FILE                          INPUT
 5.     CHECK DATE                              CALCULATE
 6.     PRINT HEADINGS                          OUTPUT
```

```
 7.    PRINT NAME + ADDRESS                    OUTPUT
 8.    ACCUMULATE RECORD COUNT                 CALCULATE
 9.    CHECK RECORD COUNT                      CALCULATE
10.    REPORT ANY ERROR                        OUTPUT
11.    PRINT END OF REPORT                     OUTPUT
12.    CLOSE CUST FILE                         OUTPUT
13.    CLOSE PRINT FILE                        OUTPUT
14.    END                                     STOP
```

By numbering each operation the structure diagram can be further expanded as shown in Fig. 3.14.

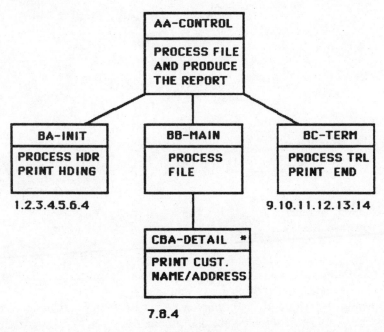

Fig. 3.14

Reads: This structured method follows the well known 'read ahead' principle. It may not always seem natural to code in this way but it does produce a clearer overall program foundation. The rule basically says, 'read after a file open and after processing a record'.

Use the desk-checking method to 'quality assure' your design at this stage. Once you begin coding it is a little too late to begin making changes!

Pseudo-code and code

We are nearly there! If the previous steps have been applied properly then this step is almost a formality.

We code using the three basic control structures of Sequence, Selection and Iteration. So, referring back to our structure chart, we obtain Fig. 3.15.

```
AA sequence
   do 1

   BA sequence
      do 2
      do 3
      do 4
      do 5
      do 6
      do 4
   BA end

   BB sequence
      CBA iterates while not EOF
         do 7
         do 8
         do 4
      CBA end
   BB end

   BC sequence
      do 9
      do 10
      do 11
      do 12
      do 13
   BC end

   do 14
AA end
```

Fig. 3.15

This notation can look a little daunting at first. However, once the basic concepts are learnt, it is actually quite simple to follow.

Sequence, for example, is simply a series of events surrounded by 'Sequence' and 'End'. Some people add indentation lines to highlight each control structure as shown in Fig. 3.16.

```
BA sequence
I    do 2
I    do 3
I    do 4
I    do 5
I    do 6
I    do 4
BA end

BB sequence
I    CBA iterates while not EOF
I    I    do 7
I    I    do 8
I    I    do 4
I    CBA end
BB end
```

Fig. 3.16

The sequence BA begins by doing instruction 2, then 3, 4, 5 and so on until the sequence ends. Next the BB control structure takes effect. BB immediately initiates the CBA control structure which iterates through 7,8,4,7,8,4,7,8,4 until the EOF condition becomes true.

The program structure now exists. Adding pseudo-code produces Fig. 3.17.

```
AA sequence
    do 1.     BEGIN.

    BA sequence
        do 2.     OPEN CUSTOMER FILE.
        do 3.     OPEN PRINT FILE.
        do 4.     READ CUSTOMER FILE.
        do 5.     CHECK DATE >= 4 MONTHS.
        do 6.     PRINT REPORT HEADINGS.
        do 4.     READ CUSTOMER FILE.
    BA end

    BB sequence
        CBA iterates while not EOF
            do 7.     PRINT NAME AND ADDRESS.
            do 8.     ADD 1 TO RECORD COUNT.
            do 4.     READ CUSTOMER FILE.
        CBA end
    BB end

    BC sequence
        do 9.     RECORD COUNT MATCHES HEADER.
        do 10.    PRINT ANY ERROR MESSAGE.
        do 11.    PRINT 'END OF REPORT'.
        do 12.    CLOSE CUSTOMER FILE.
        do 13.    CLOSE PRINT FILE.
    BC end

        do 14.    STOP RUN.
AA end
```

Fig. 3.17

Study the example above. You might be asking yourself whether 5. and 9. are Selection structures or not. Indeed they are but for the sake of simplicity they have been considered as sequences with the transition to selection being made at the time of actual coding. While not strictly correct, they have been used for the sake of example as shown in Fig. 3.18.

```
PROCEDURE DIVISION.
AA-CONTROL SECTION.
A00-ENTRY.
    PERFORM BA-INIT.
    PERFORM BB-MAIN.
    PERFORM BC-TERM.
    STOP RUN
AA99-EXIT.
    EXIT.
```

continued

Fig. 3.18

```
******************************************************
*           I N I T I A L I S A T I O N             *
******************************************************
   BA-INIT SECTION.
   BA00-ENTRY.
      OPEN INPUT   CUSTOMER-FILE.
      OPEN OUTPUT  PRINT-FILE.

      READ CUSTOMER-FILE
          AT END ......

      IF HRD-DATE > WS-ADJUSTED-DATE
          ..........

      READ CUSTOMER-FILE
          AT END ......
   BA99-EXIT.
      EXIT.


******************************************************
*           M A I N                                 *
******************************************************
   BB-MAIN SECTION.
   BB00-ENTRY.

      PERFORM CBA-DETAIL UNTIL WS-EOF.

   BB99-EXIT.
      EXIT.


******************************************************
*           T E R M I N A T I O N                   *
******************************************************
   BC-TERM SECTION.
   BC00-ENTRY.
      IF HDR-COUNT NOT EQUAL WS-COUNT
          .......
          GO TO BC99-EXIT.

      MOVE WS-END TO PRINT-LINE.
      WRITE PRINT-LINE AFTER ADVANCING 2.

      CLOSE CUSTOMER-FILE.
      CLOSE PRINT-FILE.
   BC99-EXIT.
      EXIT.


******************************************************
*           P R I N T    D E T A I L S              *
******************************************************
   CBA-DETAIL SECTION.
   CBA00-ENTRY.

      MOVE CUST-NO TO WS-CUST-NO.
      MOVE CUST-NAME TO WS-CUST-NAME.
      MOVE WS-NO-NAME-REC TO PRINT-LINE.
      WRITE PRINT-LINE AFTER ADVANCING 2.
```

Fig. 3.18 *continued*

```
MOVE SPACES TO PRINT-LINE.
MOVE CUST-ADDRESS TO WS-ADDRESS.
MOVE WS-ADDRESS TO PRINT-LINE.
WRITE PRINT-LINE AFTER ADVANCING 1.

   ADD 1 TO WS-COUNT.
CBA99-EXIT.
   EXIT.
```

Fig. 3.18 *continued*

Limitations of JSP; problems of structure clash

JSP is based on the structure of the data. It follows, therefore, that if the input and output data structures are not naturally in a form that provides the correspondences needed to derive the program structure, there will be difficulty in arriving at the form needed to produce the program.

The phenomenon which gives rise to the problem is called structure clash.

Forms of structure clash

When we introduced the idea of correspondence between input and output data structures, it was stated that it is essential that there be both the same sequence and the same number of occurrences of data component between corresponding items. If either of these conditions is not met, then it is defined as a structure clash; if the sequence is at fault, it is called an order clash; and if the number of occurrences of the data is at fault, it is called a boundary clash. These two cases will now be examined.

Order clash

Figure 3.19 shows the input and output data structures for a system. The

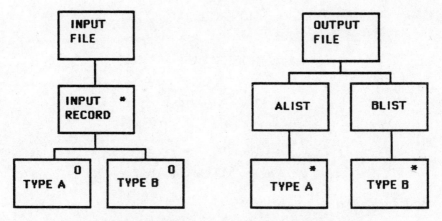

Fig. 3.19 Input and output showing order clash

input is from a serial file which contains records which may be of either type A or type B; they are filed in random order. The output required is a listing of type A records followed by type B records.

Although there are the same number of records in the input and output files, the order is different; and a correspondence cannot be drawn between the type A records or the type B records in the two structures.

A number of options are presented:

(1) The input file can be processed twice, the first run producing the type A records for output and the second producing the type B.
(2) The input file can be sorted using the record type as the primary key. It can then be processed once to produce the required listing.
(3) The whole input file can be read into RAM and accessed directly.

Option 3 can be rejected on the grounds of memory size (although this is changing as time passes and RAM sizes increase). We are left therefore with the first two options.

There are arguments in favour of both alternatives. Option (1) is probably quicker since it requires only the two runs through the data set. Sorting the file, as required by option (2), will almost certainly take more time than would be required by the second pass through the file.

However, which of the options is chosen is, in fact, of secondary relevance to this discussion. What is important is that the problem of order clash can be resolved without too much difficulty. Assuming that the option of sorting the file is chosen, Fig. 3.20 shows the procedure for resolving the order clash. This method of approach is often used in systems which find sorting particularly easy because it is done by a prewritten utility program (as in MSDOS) or is part of the implementation (as in COBOL).

INPUT FILE

SORT PROGRAM

SORTED FILE

LISTING PROGRAM

OUTPUT FILE

Fig. 3.20 Resolution of order clash

Boundary clash

To illustrate the problem of boundary clash, consider the following system.

A company holds a file of orders, each of which may contain a number of items, which may range from one or two up to several hundred.

Orders are held in a serial file. Each order consists of a record containing customer details followed by a second record holding up to 75 ordered pairs of item codes and quantities ordered, as below:

Bytesmith, 52, High St, Ilford
0123,24,0432,4,9874,45,8234,6,0654,27 ...

A report is required which lists the orders in detail; that is, lists of all the items on all of the orders in an expanded form giving the item description, unit cost and item cost. (The description and unit cost are looked up in a direct access file.) A typical section of the report would look as follows:

Bytesmith 52 High St Ilford
0123	Floppy disk	24	1.25	30.00
0432	PC Clone 1 mb RAM	4	299.50	1198.00
9874	Syllablestar	45	99.99	4499.55
8234	Printer ribbon	6	15.00	90.00

Since there are several hundred orders to be processed at any time and since many of them are short, it is decided not to print them one to a page but

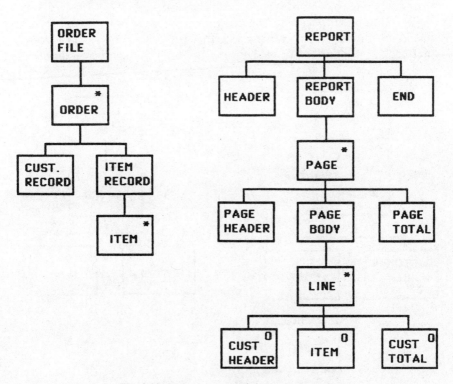

Fig. 3.21 Data structures for report program

to fill each page, giving the customer total at the end of each order and the running total at the end of each page. The report will also have a header giving the date of the run and a summary giving the total number of orders processed, the total number of items and the total value. The input and output data structures are shown in Fig. 3.21.

This problem requires some careful attention.

The next action is to look for correspondences between the input and output data structures. Well, we have the repeated component, item, in both structures and, obviously, there will be the same number of items in the input as in the output.

But the rules for correspondence say that the number of occurrences of a sub-component within a component must be the same throughout the structure; and here we come to a difficulty.

The difficulty arises from the fact that in the input structure the component, item, occurs within the item record while in the output structure it occurs within line. Since item body can contain any number of item records, we are faced with the fact that we have different numbers of occurrences in the two structures. This is known as a boundary clash.

There is no possibility of altering the data structures because there is no fixed ratio of orders per page or pages per order. That is, there may be several orders on a page or an order may occupy several pages.

The solution to the clash is similar to that used for the order clash; similar, that is, in the use of an intermediate file. It is necessary to provide an intermediate structure which will correspond to both the input and output data structures.

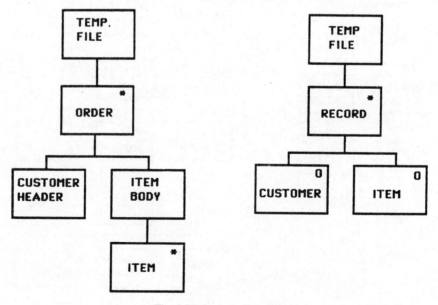

Fig. 3.22 Intermediate file

To decide how to go about this, it is necessary to choose which component of the data is the one for which the correspondence should be sought. A convenient item to pick is the line of output which corresponds to either an order header or an item in the input. The intermediate file will therefore consist of records which are either order headers or order items.

Once the intermediate file has been constructed, it can be used in two programs, one to convert data from the input structure to the intermediate structure and the other to convert from the intermediate to the output. It follows that the structure of the intermediate file will appear different to the two programs. This is illustrated in Fig. 3.22.

This file gives correspondence between both the input and output data structures, and the boundary clash is thus resolved. The correspondences are shown in Figs 3.23 and 3.24.

It should be noted once again that an alternative solution to the boundary clash problem is to read the whole of the input file into main memory and then to process it as a simple text file. We are still assuming that such a process is not feasible, the file size prohibiting the loading of it all at once. However, as mentioning earlier, the rapid and continuing growth of memory sizes available on modern systems is such that a solution which reads a whole file becomes less and less unreasonable. As the size of RAM moves inexorably into the multi-megabyte range – already common on the so-called super-minis, let alone the mainframe systems – so the size which can be accommodated will increase. It is unlikely that we will see for a long time, if

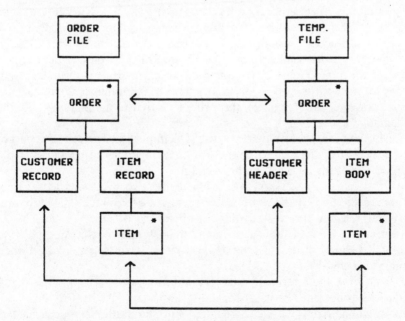

Fig. 3.23 Correspondence between input and intermediate files

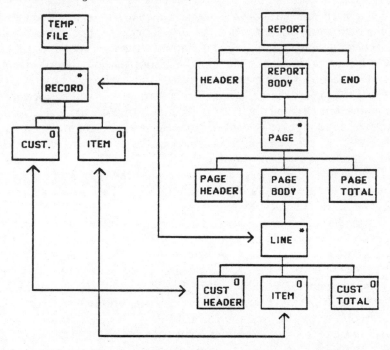

Fig. 3.24 Correspondence between intermediate and output files

ever, the largest files being accommodated in this way but, as a solution to the problems involving medium-sized files, it begins to approach feasibility.

Now that the correspondences for the two pairs of data structures can be drawn (that is, between the input and the intermediate data structures and between the intermediate and output data structures), the problem is solved.

We may now draw two program structures by combining the pairs of data structures and can complete the process with the action lists and the schematic logic.

These activities are left as an exercise. The important aspect of this part of the treatment of the topic is to indicate that the apparent obstacles to the application of the method can be overcome.

In fact, it is unnecessary to implement the two programs as separate processes and they can be combined by means of a technique called program inversion which is omitted here for reasons of space.

We now have a COBOL program that should work. Although the example is simple, it should serve to illustrate the basic stages involved when using the method.

Many think the approach is perfect and flawless. It certainly has many dedicated followers. Perhaps the most important aspect for any large department is that of a well structured but standardised approach. The arguments are many, in many directions. Form your own opinions and reach your own conclusions. Books exist that go into more detail of the Jackson approach – if you are interested then go to your local library to learn more.

Summary

The guidelines for the data structured approach are as follows:

(1) Identify the data involved.
(2) Define the data structures.
    (a) Sequence.
    (b) Selection.
    (c) Iteration.
    (d) There should be an equal number of appearances for each data item.
    (e) These data items should be able to be handled at the same time.
(3) Create the program structure around these.
    (a) Create a program segment for each 'correspondence' in the data structure.
    (b) Include a segment for all processed input 'non-corresponding' items.
    (c) Include a segment for all processed output 'non-corresponding' items.
(4) Define the program functions.
(5) Pseudo-code and code.

Exercise

Formalised data structured programming

(1) Define the major structures and make examples.

(2) Design and code the outline of the following program using the stages outlined above.

'A program to process a stock file, printing a line for every stock with a low stock level otherwise updating the file with a 'stock ok' marker'.

CHAPTER 4

Program characteristics

When you write a COBOL program you read the program specification, design your program and begin coding. Of course it is not quite as simple as that but those should be your basic thoughts when programming. That is not the end of the story however – you will have made a further assumption, revolving around the 'type' of application you are programming for, i.e. you will have placed in your mind a basic picture of the finished product and the way it will operate.

Such thoughts will be strongly influenced by the characteristics of the program, these will fall into a number of basic categories; on-line, interactive, batch update, batch report and database. Each type has different requirements and considerations ranging from the way the program is specified, designed, programmed and implemented.

The category of program should point you in a particular direction. As you gain experience you will automatically approach the design and programming task in a particular way. For a number of more common application types, we will consider a recommended approach to take and pointers and considerations to bear in mind. Remember that you cannot always assume that the program specification provided will provide the total solution. On occasions you will be required to adopt the analyst/programmer rule, making reasoned decisions based on what you read, see and hear.

On-line

On-line programs are designed to be used via a visual display unit or screen. They allow a user to use a screen and keyboard to transact with a program.

Such on-line applications require a design consideration from at least two angles – that of the user and that of the person supporting the application. For example, from a user point of view a screen should be easy to understand and navigate around. From a support point of view, any screen design should include the program name running it. When problems occur the program name can be quoted, quickly directing the programmer where to begin looking in order to solve any problems, see Fig. 4.1.

A common technique nowadays is to create menu-driven systems. Users

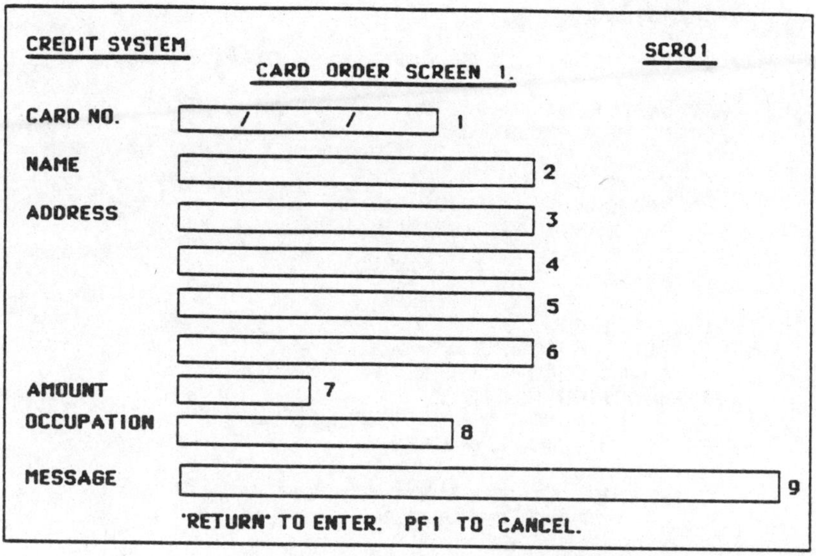

```
CREDIT SYSTEM                                          SCRO1
                    CARD ORDER SCREEN 1.

    CARD NO.      [    /        /        ]  1

    NAME          [                        ]  2

    ADDRESS       [                        ]  3

                  [                        ]  4

                  [                        ]  5

                  [                        ]  6

    AMOUNT        [        ]  7
    OCCUPATION    [                    ]  8

    MESSAGE       [                            ]  9

              'RETURN' TO ENTER.  PF1 TO CANCEL.
```

VALIDATION ON A DATA ENTRY SCREEN

Fig. 4.1

are presented with a list of possible options usually numbered from one upwards with one option per line. Selections can be made either by entering the option number and pressing return or using the cursor keys to pinpoint the required option and pressing return. Such techniques can be applied to any application and are almost a prerequisite now in systems design, see Fig. 4.2.

```
              CUSTOMER ORDERING SYSTEM            CUO1

    Date   99/99/99                       Time   99:99


          1. Enquire on an Order.

          2. Create a new Order.

          3. Enquire on Customer Credit details.

          4. Dispatch Catalogue request.

          5. Dispatch Customer Statement request.

          6. EXIT.

              Option [9]

  Message Line    xxxxxxxxxxxxxxxxxxxxxxxxxxxxxxxxxxxxxxxx
```

Fig. 4.2   *continued*

```
   BC40-GET-OPTION.
*
*  GET OPTION.  IF VALID PROCESS, ELSE DISPLAY MESSAGE.
*
       MOVE SPACE TO WS-OPTION.
       ACCEPT WS-OPTION.

       IF WS-OPTION = 1
           PERFORM CA-ENQUIRE-ORDER
           GO TO BC40-GET-OPTION.
       IF WS-OPTION = 2
           PERFORM CB-CREATE-ORDER
           GO TO BC40-GET-OPTION.
       IF WS-OPTION = 3
           PERFORM CC-CREDIT-ENQUIRE
           GO TO BC40-GET-OPTION.
       IF WS-OPTION = 4
           PERFORM CD-CATALOGUE-REQUEST
           GO TO BC40-GET-OPTION.
       IF WS-OPTION = 5
           PERFORM CE-STATEMENT-REQUEST
           GO TO BC40-GET-OPTION.
       IF WS-OPTION = 6
           GO TO BC99-EXIT.

   BC50-INVALID-OPTION.
       MOVE "INVALID OPTION - MUST BE 1 TO 6 ".
       DISPLAY SCREEN.

       GO TO BC40-GET-OPTION.
```

Fig. 4.2 *continued*

From the system point of view the use of menus should be encouraged. Detail the program name and system name on a particular part of the screen, across all programs. Give the screen a descriptive title. Group like data types together and properly annotate the screen – you cannot assume the user will understand the meaning of every acronym, abbreviation etc. Do not make the screen too cluttered or cumbersome to use.

Use of the keyboard is an equally important though an often neglected area of on-line program design. Consider the use of function keys if possible, the numeric keypad and so on. Again, be consistent in the use of keys across all programs. Ideally such detail should be specified at the design level, this is not always the case however.

Interactive

Interactive screen handling takes the idea of on-line programs one stage further. They are sometimes referred to as TP or Transaction Processing systems. Different manufacturers provide different facilities but the basic principles remain the same. Interactive programs allow the user to transact with the computer, usually in one of the three basic transaction types; insertion, deletion and amendment.

Screen design is again very important. The program name, system name and screen title should all be displayed. Like data items should be grouped together. The sequence of such data entry fields is important. Reference fields, for example a customer number or account number, should be placed at the top left of the screen as one of the first fields entered. The least important or least used fields should be displayed last. New techniques such as the use of bold type, inverse-video etc. ought to be employed where available if these would aid the user in viewing and comprehending such a screen.

Sometimes, due to the complexity of an application, the screen will actually be split into two or more screens. When this is the case it should be made clear to the user what screen number i.e. page one, page two . . . is being viewed. In addition, it should be possible to move backwards and forwards through 'pages' of the same screen before finally committing the transaction.

Validation is an important part of any system. Validation and verification techniques should be employed wherever applicable. These will normally include range checks, type checks etc. Error reporting should be used to notify the user of any problems e.g. a customer record not found. It is standard to use the bottom one or two lines solely for the use of error and help messages.

Possible date validation checks:

(1) Date in the correct format?
(2) Does date need to be less, equal or greater than 'today's' date?
(3) Is it a leap year?
(4) Correct number of days for the month?

Response time for on-line and interactive systems is now of predominant importance. Although machines are much faster, larger amounts of data and sophisticated systems mean that the time taken to perform a transaction is of major importance. Consider the situation whereby customers can order goods over the telephone. If the telephone clerk has to wait two minutes to receive confirmation of an order there are going to be a lot of disgruntled customers. Efficient coding and extracting of data is again a consideration – file design will play a great part in this if much cross-referencing or data access is to be performed.

Interactive systems afford the user great power but can also imply much potential damage. In addition to stringent validation checks, security must become a major issue. This can range from the use of screen passwords through to the updating of audit or transaction files, recording every transaction performed by every user and often including such details as the screen or terminal used, time, date, transaction and user identification.

An example Audit log could look as follows:

```
TIME: 99:99:99:99  DATE:  99/99/99  USER: XXXXXXXXXX
TERMINAL: 9999  TRANSACTION TYPE: XXXXXX
RECORD KEY: 9999999999  PROGRAM: XXXXXXXXX

*********************************************************

TIME: 99:99:99:99  DATE:  99/99/99  USER: XXXXXXXXXX
TERMINAL: 9999  TRANSACTION TYPE: XXXXXX
RECORD KEY: 9999999999  PROGRAM: XXXXXXXXX

*********************************************************
```

In summary the central issues include the screen design, grouping of data, design standard, on-line validation, security and response time.

Batch up-dates

Batch up-dates used to be the main method of processing files between five and fifteen years ago. The basic principle involves a master file of mainly static data and a transaction file holding transactions i.e. deletions, insertions and amendments. The transaction file was run against the master file, matching records and producing a third file, the new master file.

With the use nowadays of indexed files, database systems and interactive systems the idea of batch up-dates is not now generally applied. The principles are still used, however, on occasions. One such example is the use of remote terminals that store transactions through the day. The end-of-day processing involves down-loading the data across a communications line for batch up-dating.

Such systems were based on sorted sequential files and required programs written specifically for the purpose. These established methods relied on a number of basic principles; sorts, header and trailer records and hash totals.

Sequential files were created with header and trailer records. Each file had a header record as the first record which contained basic file details such as the file name etc. This was followed by many standard data records and finally a trailer record. The trailer record contained a number of totals known as hash totals. Whilst processing the file serially each record would be read in turn. Designated numeric fields would be designated for use in creating hash totals. Such numeric fields would be added into working-storage section fields. At the end of the file these calculated fields would be compared with existing fields on the trailer record, holding like information – any discrepancy would be reported as an error. Hash totals were a basic way in which file integrity could be verified.

Such programs should always produce a run report of some kind detailing the program and its function, any errors or discrepancies and totals of records read, checks etc. Audit trails detailing actual updates performed will sometimes be a requirement. Finally, the program should report that the program terminated successfully.

Batch report production

Batch reports are a common method of producing reports, whether run

```
WORKING-STORAGE SECTION.
*
01  WS-PAGE              PIC 9(04) VALUE ZEROES.
01  WS-LINE-COUNT        PIC 9(02) VALUE 99.
01  WS-RECORD-COUNT      PIC 9(06) VALUE ZEROES.
*
01  WS-HASH-COUNT-1      PIC 9(06) VALUE ZEROES.
01  WS-HASH-COUNT-2      PIC 9(06) VALUE ZEROES.
*
*  PRINT FILE DESCRIPTION.
*
01  WS-HEADING1              PIC X(60) VALUE
    "STK1.   S T O C K     R E P O R T".
01  WS-UNDERLINE1           PIC X(60) VALUE
    " ===========================".
*
01  WS-DATE-PAGE.
    03  WSD-DAY          PIC Z9    VALUE ZEROES.
    03  FILLER           PIC X     VALUE "/".
    03  WSD-MONTH        PIC 99    VALUE ZEROES.
    03  FILLER           PIC X     VALUE "/".
    03  WSD-YEAR         PIC 99    VALUE ZEROES.
    03  FILLER           PIC X(60) VALUES SPACES.
    03  FILLER           PIC X(10) VALUE
        "  PAGE :   ".
    03  WSD-PAGE         PIC ZZZ9  VALUE ZEROES.
*
01  WS-HEADING2.
    03  FILLER              PIC X(30) VALUE
        "STOCK NUMBER            ".
    03  FILLER              PIC X(30) VALUE
        "STOCK NAME              ".
    03  FILLER              PIC X(30) VALUE
        "STOCK LEVEL    REORDER LEVEL ".
*
*
01  WS-DETAIL1.
    03  WSD-STOCK-NUMBER    PIC 9(6)  VALUE ZEROES.
    03  FILLER              PIC X(24) VALUE SPACES.
    03  WSD-STOCK-NAME      PIC X(25) VALUE SPACES.
    03  FILLER              PIC X(05) VALUE SPACES.
    03  WSD-STOCK-LEVEL     PIC ZZZZ9 VALUE ZEROES.
    03  FILLER              PIC X(10) VALUE SPACES.
    03  WSD-REORDER-LEVEL   PIC ZZZZ9 VALUE ZEROES.
*
01  WS-PRINT-END           PIC X(132) VALUE
    "END OF REPORT: STK1".
*
```

Fig. 4.3

overnight or simply in a batch processing queue. Whilst users will often want to interrogate or update via a screen, they will usually want to refer to hard-copy paper reports.

Fast line printers are commonly used but additional methods now include the use of high quality laser printers, graphics printers and colour printers. Despite all this new science the most common report will be that of the 132 column line-printer produced variety. With this in mind it is possible to provide some basic guidelines on programming such reports in COBOL.

There are two basic considerations when writing report programs – the use of COBOL and the format of the actual report itself.

The first consideration when programming report applications should be the attention paid to the working-storage section. There will be a temptation to use the 'continuation' symbol in column seven to produce lengthy print line descriptions. Avoid the temptation – such declarations are difficult to code and even worse to maintain or enhance. For example, a 120 character print line should be coded as two lines of 60 characters. Subsequent maintenance would then be far easier in terms of working out spacings.

Group like print lines together and use one 01 level per print line. Include comments and describe 01 levels as header lines or detail lines. Avoid clever programming that describes more than one possible print line in the same 01 level, see Fig. 4.3.

Keep such particulars simple and maintainable. In the procedure division use sections to print like items such as report titles or detail lines. Finally, always print titles as part of the initialisation so that in the event of program failure some record of its running is produced.

Every report page should include basic header information including the program name, report title, page number and date, see Fig. 4.4. Minor header information should be at the left- or right-hand side while titles

```
Stock System                                        Page  99999
STK03                                               Date 99/99/99


                              STOCK  REPORT
                              =============


    Stock ID        Item            Quantity        Description
    --------        ----            --------        -----------

    XXXXXXX         XXXXXXXXXXXXXX  9999999         XXXXXXXXXXXXXX
    XXXXXXX         XXXXXXXXXXXXXX  9999999         XXXXXXXXXXXXXXX
    XXXXXXX         XXXXXXXXXXXXXX  9999999         XXXXXXXXXXXXXXX
    XXXXXXX         XXXXXXXXXXXXXX  9999999         XXXXXXXXXXXXXXX




                           END  OF  REPORT
```

Fig. 4.4

should be centred. On the last report page it should be indicated that the report has finished e.g. printing 'End of Report'. Imagine what the consequences would be if the last page went missing and there was no obvious means of detecting such a disaster!

Basic layout can be the make-or-break of any report. Make use of blank lines, align fields and include column headings and totals where appropriate. Underline titles where necessary. Again group like items together in a reasoned and logical manner.

Database programs

Database systems are becoming more and more prolific. The three main database architectures all have their own supported mainframe systems. Although such systems come with an abundance of utilities and tools to select and report on data, COBOL still has a major part to play in manipulating such extracted information.

The most common method of handling such arrangements is to embed the database selection commands into ordinary COBOL programs. Such embedded commands are treated in a similar way to the earlier principal of embedding calls to the operating system. The most prolific database query language is SQL (Sequential Query Language), described in more detail later. Normally a special declaration division will be present to describe special variables etc. otherwise the code will be very similar to any ordinary COBOL program. Data can be selected or updated and then handled in the normal way.

Database programs are discussed in Part 2.

Summary

To summarise, the five basic program types are: on-line, interactive, batch update, batch report and database.

When writing such programs consider the following:

On-line

(1) Menus
(2) Program/system name on screen
(3) Group like items
(4) Consider the keyboard
(5) Keep it simple

Interactive

(1) Validation

(2) Security
(3) Response time

Batch updates

(1) Integrity checks
(2) Progress reporting

Batch report production

(1) Printer type
(2) Keep working-storage simple/maintainable
(3) Detail basic report header information
(4) Consider the report layout – plan it

Database programs

(1) Selection/update statements are embedded
(2) Include relevant comments

CHAPTER 5
Programming standards

Programming standards, when implemented sensibly, provide a necessary steering factor across all programs written. So what are 'programming standards' exactly?

Such standards provide guidelines on how to structure a program, which columns to position particular statements, naming conventions for data items etc.

Clearly, programming standards are going to be useful only if people are self motivated in using them – too many standards and they will be ignored or confused, too few and they provide little real benefit. What is required is a sensible series of guidelines applicable to each division of the COBOL language. Each standard should have an identifiable reason behind it so that those using the standards convince themselves of their value.

The basic rules therefore are; create a practical but effective set of standards, convince those using them of their worth, use them!

What follows is an example set of programming standards that could be tailored to the particular requirements of any company's computer department.

An example of programming standards

ABC COMPANY PLC

COBOL PROGRAMMING STANDARDS

1989

Contents

(1) Introduction
(2) Identification Division
(3) Structure
(4) Messages
(5) Working Storage
(6) Procedure Division

Introduction

These standards have been written to define guidelines for the writing of COBOL programs at ABC. These standards should be used every time program development or maintenance takes place.

Any queries should be directed to the System Manager.

Identification Division

The IDENTIFICATION DIVISION must be included at the beginning of each program. Details should include:

The Program ID,
Author's name,
Date written.

Also included should be a brief description of what the program does and the section structure.

In addition, an outline 'modification box' should be included. This must be updated whenever program changes are made and should include the following:

Modification number,
Nature of change,
Date and author,
New version number.

Structure

Each program should be written as logical steps represented by COBOL Sections. These Sections should only be performed by higher sections. Paragraphs must not be performed.

The program structure should be defined in the Identification Division, e.g. see Fig. 5.1.

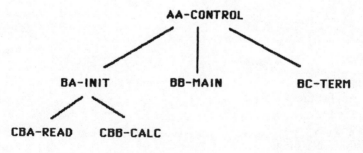

Fig. 5.1

To clarify, the first letter represents the level, the second letter represents the calling level and the third level represents the sequence within the level.

Sensible SECTION names must be used to compliment the structuring conventions. Prefixes and numbers should be used in conjunction with descriptive names, to describe section and paragraph names. Order by ascending alphanumerics, see Fig. 5.2.

```
PROCEDURE DIVISION.
AA-CONTROL SECTION.
A00-ENTRY.
        PERFORM BA-INIT.
        PERFORM BB-MAIN.
        PERFORM BC-TERM.
AA99-EXIT.
        EXIT.
BA-INIT SECTION.
BA00-ENTRY.

        OPEN INPUT   CUST-FILE.
        OPEN OUTPUT PRINT-FILE.
BA10-READ.
        PERFORM CA-READ.
BA20-DATES.
        ACCEPT WS-DATE FROM .......

BA99-EXIT.
        EXIT.
```

Fig. 5.2

Messages

All error conditions must be reported with appropriate detail i.e. nature of error, section and paragraph name, key of record, input–output operation etc.

Working Storage

All like items of working storage should be grouped together. Comments should be used where required.

Level numbers should begin with 01 and be increased by two each time i.e. 01, 03, 05, 07 etc. Each level should be indented by four spaces. PIC statements should always be aligned where possible.

```
01   WS-DATE.
     03   WS-DD        PIC 99.
     03   WS-MM        PIC 99.
     03   WS-YY        PIC 99.
```

All working storage data items should be prefixed by the letters WS. In addition, all items should be initialised using the VALUE clause.

Level 77 should not be used – some compilers no longer support them and they are considered inefficient.

Procedure Division

The Procedure Division should be made up of a number of performed sections. Each section should include a section header detailing the purpose of the section. All sections should be kept to a manageable size, generally no longer than two pages maximum.

Prefixes for section names should be used with all sections in alphanumeric order. Blank lines should be used to space statements, paragraphs and sections.

Only sections should be performed and not paragraphs. Paragraphs within the same section can be subject to GO TO statements. Minimise the use of backward GO TOs or those that span many statements. Avoid complex versions of the Perform statement.

Include in the initialisation section a DISPLAY to output the current program version number – this should be amended after each program change.

Indentation should be used for conditional statements.

```
IF   WS-MONTH > 12
     MOVE 1 TO WS-MONTH
ELSE
     PERFORM DA-PROCESS-MONTH.
```

Avoid the use of nested IFs which create maintenance problems. Use no more than two levels of nested IFs.

Code one statement per line. Keep the code simple.

Use brackets in arithmetic statements.

On any input–output operation use the full verb to detect and report error conditions. Use separate subroutine sections to perform input–output operations. Such sections should be prefixed with an 'S'.

```
****************************************************
*         R E A D    C U S T    F I L E
*
****************************************************
 SI-READ-CUST SECTION.
 SI00.
     MOVE "N" TO WS-CUST-NOT-FOUND.

     READ CUST-FILE
         INVALID KEY
         MOVE "Y" TO WS-CUST-NOT-FOUND
         DISPLAY "CUST READ ERROR KEY= "
         CUST-KEY.
 SI99-EXIT.
     EXIT.
```

Make use of the asterisk in column 7 to include comments.

Exercise

Programming standards

There are occasions when programmers write small pieces of code to be used to test other pieces of code such as subroutines. Such sections of code are known as test harnesses.

Such testing modules are referred to as a test harness and are used to test small utilities in isolation. They take parameters as their input and pass back an output parameter. An example utility to be used by many programs could be a date checking utility. The input would be a date in a standard format and the output could be a valid or invalid indicator. For example, 310989 would return an invalid indicator as September only has 30 days!

(1) Using the standards described, write a well structured 'test harness module' to be used to test any called utility.

CHAPTER 6
Program testing

Testing is one of the most important aspects of COBOL programming within a business environment. It can be applied to at least two levels of system development; testing of a program and testing of a system.

In this chapter we examine why testing is so important, its implications and how to approach testing in a methodical and business like fashion.

Testing is all too often left until last and then not fully carried out. This approach achieves a short-term result but creates long-term problems. Do not be tempted to skimp on testing, it is just not worth it!

Why test?

To query why we should test perhaps seems such an obvious question it hardly needs asking. However, how many programs have you written that worked first time? What is even more serious is a program that appears to function correctly but in fact does not, either because its various paths have not been proved or because of some more subtle flaw. Arithmetic inaccuracies are a common error but not always easy to spot at a cursory glance.

So when a program does not work it can be for a multitude of reasons.

- Perhaps you didn't understand the program specification?
- Perhaps the person who wrote the specification did not understand the program!
- The program was badly designed and hastily coded?
- The compiler contains bugs or quirks not taken into consideration.

Whatever the reason, there remain important considerations. Successful testing will help to identify the existence of any problems. Successful testing will identify where problems exist, allow them to be corrected and proved, and document the process. Note the use of the word 'successful', for if testing is not carried out in a structured and methodical way, it is likely to prove a complete waste of time!

Unfortunately, some aspects of testing are often performed in the later stages of project development. With deadlines to be met it is often tempting to skimp on testing – do not do it. It is far better to deliver a good product late, than one that will never work, on time. If you are approaching the deadline for the program you are working on and need more time, ask for it. In making your manager aware of the problem you are taking the professional approach. To skimp on testing for whatever reason, is totally unprofessional.

Design for testing

Testing is one of the most important aspects of successful system implementation. The concept of testing a program begins even before the code is written – this approach is known as 'design for testing'.

This technique argues that a well designed and written program is easier to test and correct than a badly designed one. Give some thought to the general structure of your program before you begin coding. The use of the box diagram approach is recommended.

Box and line diagrams

Box and line diagrams are a method developed for designing and helping documenting COBOL programs. Boxes are used to identify specific functions within the program e.g. reading a record from a particular file. A top-down approach is applied so that generalised tasks become broken down to more specific actions. The concept and use of COBOL sections lends itself well to this technique. It should be apparent from the diagram as to how the basic program will perform – working left to right, top to bottom.

When program designing, begin with the name of the program, within a box at the top of the page. The three boxes below specify INITIALISATION, MAIN Processing and TERMINATION sections. MAIN Processing should further be refined into discrete actions while INITIALISATION and TERMINATION should be left as self explanatory i.e. opening and closing files etc. A concise box diagram should soon develop. Aim for a degree of detail that ensures completeness without becoming unmanageable. It soon becomes apparent how the top-down approach can simplify the definition of an initially complicated program specification.

The use of box diagrams and its relevance to testing should now be apparent. To test, one has to identify what should be tested. A box diagram will act as a documented list of actions that should be verified, see Fig. 6.1. This should be used in conjunction with the Test Plan you will create – this is discussed next.

The use of box diagrams will create a positive testing approach i.e. testing for expected events. However when testing a program, you should also allow for the unexpected type of error and take the negative approach as well. So

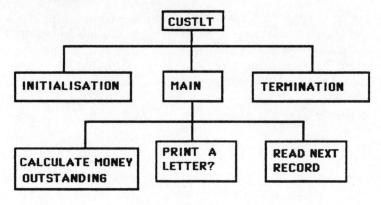

Fig. 6.1

```
BB-MAIN SECTION.
BB00-ENTRY.
    PERFORM CBA-CALC-MONEY.
    PERFORM CBB-PRINT-LETTER.
    PERFORM CBC-READ-RECORD.
BB99-EXIT.
    EXIT.


 CBA-CALC-MONEY SECTION.
 CBA00-ENTRY.
****************************************************
* CALCULATE LETTER BALANCES.
****************************************************
    MOVE CUST-BALANCE TO WS-MONEY.
    PERFORM Z10-CALC-INTEREST.
    ADD WS-INTEREST TO WS-MONEY.
    PERFORM Z20-DISCOUNT.
    SUBTRACT WS-DISCOUNT FROM WS-MONEY.
 CBA99-EXIT.
    EXIT.


 CBB-PRINT-LETTER SECTION.
 CBB00-ENTRY.
****************************************************
* PRINT A LETTER FOR THE CUSTOMER.
****************************************************
    MOVE ZERO TO WS-COUNT.

    MOVE CUST-NAME TO PR-CUST-NAME.
    MOVE WS-LINE1 TO PRINT-REC.
    WRITE PRINT-REC AFTER ADVANCING PAGE.

 CBB10-PRINT-ADDRESS.
    ADD 1 TO WS-COUNT.
    MOVE CUST-ADDRESS (WS-COUNT) TO PR-ADDRESS.
    MOVE WS-LINE2 TO PRINT-REC.
    WRITE PRINT-REC AFTER ADVANCING 1.
    IF WS-COUNT < 5
        GO TO CBB10-PRINT-ADDRESS.
```

```
CBB20.
    MOVE WS-BALANCE TO   PR-BALANCE.
    MOVE PR-BALANCE TO   PRINT-REC.
    WRITE PRINT-REC AFTER ADVANCING 5.
    MOVE WS-DISCOUNT TO PR-DISCOUNT.
    MOVE PR-DISCOUNT TO PRINT-REC.
    WRITE PRINT-REC AFTER ADVANCING 2.
    MOVE WS-INTEREST TO PR-INTEREST.
    MOVE PR-INTEREST TO PRINT-REC.
    WRITE PRINT-REC AFTER ADVANCING 2.
    MOVE WS-MONEY TO    PR-MONEY.
    MOVE PR-MONEY TO    PRINT-REC.
    WRITE PRINT-REC AFTER ADVANCING 3.
CBB99-EXIT.
    EXIT.


 CBC-READ-RECORD SECTION.
 CBC00-ENTRY.
 **************************************************
 * READ NEXT CUSTOMER RECORD. AT END OF FILE?
 **************************************************
    READ CUSTOMER-FILE
        AT END
        MOVE "Y" TO WS-EOF.
CBC99-EXIT.
    EXIT.
```

a second and almost mandatory design consideration should be to consider and then allow for those negative error conditions. Calculate what will happen if a 'Random Read' of a record fails. Should you not give some kind of warning with details of where and when the error occurred? This might seem obvious but programmers can become a little lazy! All error conditions should be accounted for.

How do I test?

Testing a program does not have to be the ill defined task it might initially appear to be. Your aim is to thoroughly test and document a COBOL program. By using a structured approach, the task can be made as simple as possible.

One of your first questions should be 'What am I testing?' What initially appears a silly question is perhaps not so stupid.

Are you testing a simple subroutine or a complete program?

Are you testing the program in a Live production or Test files environment?

Are you testing an interactive program or will it run in batch mode?

Next consider what you are trying to prove, in terms of your program testing. The following steps should be taken.

(1) Identify all paths in your code.

(2) Check the compatibility of data types and their sizes.

(3) Check input–output handling and error reporting.

(4) Check the program function against program specification.

By asking the following questions you are ready to begin testing.

Now a recommendation. As your first test, ask a colleague to review your code. This should only take about ten minutes and can prove invaluable in spotting 'obvious' mistakes e.g. missing full-stops etc. Remember, you have been staring at that code for days now and your eyes will glance over the most glaring errors. A fresh eye will often catch these errors and can prove ten minutes well invested. Offer to do the same for him as well!

Test scripts

Testing proper begins with the creation of a 'test script'. A test script is a piece of program documentation in its own right. It details the different test conditions to be checked against a particular piece of code. In use, actual against expected results are recorded.

As the outline script demonstrates, its use is almost self explanatory. The important factors are that the tests are valid and comprehensive and that you actually use a test script at all!

The following steps should be taken when creating an effective script.

(1) Detail all possible conditions.

   e.g. writing a record, validation, error handling etc. Use your box diagram for this purpose.

(2) Design test data to verify all these conditions.

   e.g. include difficult data combinations, consider program validation.

(3) Sequence your tests for efficiency and completeness in your testing.

(4) Write your test script.

In creating your test script, see Fig. 6.2, you are well on the way to successful testing.

Test data

The creation of test data is generally regarded as one of the least interesting aspects of COBOL programming! However, if it is to be used effectively, time and thought should be put into its creation.

Sometimes it will be possible to use a subset of one or more 'live' data files. On other occasions you will have to create the data from scratch. This will often be a good way of confirming your understanding of your program and the system it is to be a part of! Once created it can be useful to keep your test data in a common library ready for others to use. If this is not already done

TEST SCRIPT.   SYSTEM: PROGRAM:

TEST ID DATE	INPUT	CONDITION	EXPECTED	ACTUAL
1/7/7/89	TEST DATA	CALCULATE 3% INT.	3% INT	
2.	ZERO BAL.	CALCULATE BALS.	ZEROES PRODUCED.	
3.	TEST DATA	CALCULATE DISC.	2% DISC.	
4.	TEST DATA	PRINT NAME & ADDRESS.	CORRECTLY PRINTED.	
5.	TEST DATA	PRINTING FIGURES.	FIGURES CORRECT.	
6.	TEST DATA	LETTER OK.	PAGE THROWS OK.	
7.	TEST DATA	READ RECORD	RECORD READ.	
8.	TEST DATA	END OF FILE	PROCESSING ENDS.	

Fig. 6.2

then suggest it to your manager. Alternatively put forth the idea of a complete test system. This complete set of test files will help to ensure data integrity across data files and would can time.

If you do have to create your own test data, be prepared to give the exercise thought and consideration. Refer to your test plan. Consider the way your program should be working. Does it expect data in a particular order? If so, include unordered data as a test. When generating numeric test data think about including negative numbers, large numbers or very small numbers – will your program handle such rogue data sensibly? Consider the users who will be operating your program. What sort of mistakes are they likely to make? Consider times and dates. Does your program handle leap years or the year 2000? Try testing for rounding errors. If your program produces a report then ensure you have enough data to generate at least one page throw and so on.

The volume of test data will be influenced by the type of program being tested. Batch programs could require a hundred or more test records. Volumes very much depend on the application but better too much than too little. Interactive programs are generally easier to size. Specific conditions need to be tested for specific 'transactions' e.g. insertion, deletion, amendment. Remember that test data will include which keys to press in this situation.

Do not be tempted to economise on effort at this stage. If the task of generating such data becomes difficult then seek the advice and guidance of an experienced colleague. A second opinion will often provide fresh input. Finally, document all test data produced. This should include a before and after view of the information.

Possible test data:

```
MR.L SMITH    45,THE LANE    LUTON       HERTS    00067.67
MRS.JONES     1,THE ROAD     BEDS                 00100.50
PETER BROWN   76A,THE GREEN  ST.ALBANS           -00345.00
MRS.STEVENS   23,OLD VILLA   OXEY        BEDS     99999.99
```

Testing

When you begin testing, consider what you are testing. If you are testing a subroutine you can use the concept of designing and writing a 'test harness'. This is a small piece of code designed to accept parameters into your subroutine and report on the output of your subroutine. The test harness itself should be tested of course. Conversely, if you are testing an interactive program as opposed to a batch program, testing considerations will differ. On-line screen printers can be useful in documenting interactive program testing. In addition, rigorous documenting of all tests should be documented including the recording of keys pressed, their sequence, screen beeps etc. – batch program report tests are therefore much simpler to document!

It is important that all test results are documented on the test script. Be sure to include any output produced such as error reports, program reports and file listings. Such documentation is useful to whoever signs off the program, and the maintenance programmer possibly called to amend the program later in its life, see Fig. 6.3.

A structured approach as detailed will help formalise the process. To re-iterate the basic steps:

(1) Design your program for testing.
(2) Identify all paths and conditions in your program.
(3) Create your test data.
(4) Write the test script.
(5) Test your program against your test script.
(6) Detail test data used – before and after.
(7) Amend your program where required and re-test.

TEST SCRIPT.   SYSTEM: PROGRAM:

TEST ID DATE	INPUT	CONDITION	EXPECTED	ACTUAL

Fig. 6.3

Exercise

Program testing

(1) Produce a personal checklist for program testing.

(2) As an exercise, find a book on decision tables and think how they could be used in program testing.

CHAPTER 7
Structured walkthroughs

Structured walkthroughs are a technique used on large projects to review a piece of work. Structured walkthroughs can occur at any point in a project and can be used to look at many different aspects of a project. Sometimes it might be the results of the design stage being reviewed, alternatively and perhaps more relevant, it could be a program that is under discussion. Such events, whenever performed, should be seen as a positive opportunity to learn and evaluate an element of work.

Structured walkthroughs will generally involve several members of a project team, all of whom should be peers of the person whose code is under review. Three to five people is not an unreasonable number, with the meeting being pre-arranged and held in a room conducive to the activity. The basic idea of a structured walkthrough is to allow a group of like-minded and experienced people to consider a piece of work in a constructive and professional manner. It will generally be the author of the work under discussion who presents the work. Other members can then comment, query etc. the work with a view to picking up any errors, inconsistencies, lack of programming standards and so on.

Walkthroughs can be and sometimes are viewed as an opportunity to criticise or 'pull to bits' someone else's efforts. Alternatively there can be a tendency for the person who wrote the reviewed program to view it as sacred, any criticism being a personal attack on their work. Both perspectives are wrong – the objective is simply to produce a better product by pooling resources. Indeed, much can often be learnt by discussing other people's ideas or approaches to work. Just as importantly, serious errors may be detected that could have a major impact if not uncovered.

```
PROGRAM IN ->    WALKTHROUGH USING    ->    BETTER
                 A PEER GROUP.              PROGRAM OUT.
```

To summarise, structured walkthroughs are designed to find errors or inconsistencies in a piece of work – in this case a COBOL program. They are conducted by a small group of peers led by the person whose work is under review. The aim is not to be critical or derogatory, merely to be constructive by spotting what might otherwise go unnoticed.

So, how should a structured walkthrough be organised and managed? We consider these questions next.

Any walkthrough should always be pre-arranged at a time to suit all members. A careful balance should be maintained so as not to hold such events too often or too infrequently. Time is money and time spent in such a way is going to impact on any time schedules, the advantage however being that time spent finding errors during structured walkthroughs now will be time saved later. Everyone present should want to be present and understand the reason for holding such meetings. Discussion material should be circulated shortly before the meeting to allow everyone involved time to familiarise themselves with the discussion material. For those not familiar with structured walkthroughs, time should be given to explaining the purpose and general outline of such a meeting.

As with any meeting basic rules should be applied. Book a room well in advance having made sure that everyone required will be available to attend. Make everyone aware of the time and location. Circulate all code to be walked-through. Keep to a schedule. Too long a meeting and people lose interest and the meeting becomes worthless. An hour as a maximum is a good duration to aim for. Finally, be sure that everyone is aware of his or her role in the meeting.

For a structured walkthrough to be successful everyone must know their role. The first role to consider and the most important is that of the chairman. They will play a large part in such a meeting and can turn a potential success into failure, and vice versa. The second role is that of the scribe or recorder. This person, as the name obviously suggests, has the responsibility of noting the salient points raised during the meeting. Finally, others can be present whose only task is to discuss the program in question.

The chairman has a difficult task. With personalities as variable as they often are, they must ensure that walkthrough remains a controlled and productive affair. Meetings, if not properly managed, can soon degenerate into shouting matches. Conversely, the chairman should also make sure that everyone makes their opinion known. It is all too easy to allow the stronger personalities to dominate, not because their ideas are any more valid, but simply because it is the loudest voices that tend to get heard!

The basic objective of the meeting must be the chairman's goal i.e. to allow all members present the opportunity to debate possible errors, ambiguities and misunderstandings in a controlled atmosphere. Remember, however, that the chairman's task begins as soon as the idea of a walkthrough has been agreed, i.e. distributing discussion material, organising a meeting place and communicating the fact – no small undertaking.

The scribe has an equally important, though less obvious, role to play. No matter how constructive an exchange of views, if no one can remember the conclusions then the meeting has been an almost total waste of time. The scribe should be responsible for noting a number of items. Basic documentation should include the date and venue, those present and the

THE   CHAIRMAN

THE SCRIBE | THE PROGRAM | YOU AND YOUR
                  |_____| PROGRAM

TEAM MEMBER 1.   TEAM MEMBER 2.   TEAM MEMBER 3.

piece of work under review. Specifically, points to be noted are action points generated from dialogue – the name of the person who raised the point should also be noted.

After the meeting any errors raised should be scheduled for investigation and possible correction. Again, if no action is taken then the meeting will generally be regarded as a waste of time.

Such events can produce many subtle benefits. It may be that for some of the more junior members of staff, this is the first formal meeting that they have ever attended – a sense of 'want' and professionalism results. Everyone should leave the meeting having drawn positive conclusions. Such events are a very worthwhile exercise.

In summary, points to consider for a successful walkthrough are:

(1) Organise properly in advance.
(2) Circulate discussion material before-hand.
(3) Appoint roles.
(4) Control the meeting.
(5) Note all actions.
(6) Keep to a reasonable timescale.
(7) Act on points raised.

A walkthrough

So, the room has been booked, the participants informed and discussion material circulated. The team leader is acting as chairman with three programmers, one of whom is also the scribe.

To begin with, the scribe records members present, date and purpose of the meeting. The chairman checks that everyone is ready and has a copy of the program under discussion.

Why are we all here? What is the objective of this meeting?

The chairman states that under review is a screen customer enquiry program written in COBOL. The objective of the meeting is to review the code's structure and, more specifically, invite suggestions on how to improve the program's speed and performance when in use. The scribe records this.

Everyone has looked through the program source code. First to be mentioned by one of the younger analysts is the fact that a table with an OCCURS of 100 is initialised before each screen enquiry. Is this necessary and does the table need to be so big? The chairman comments that the table should be initialised every time but only needs to have an OCCURS of 20. The scribe notes this fact.

Another of the programmers notes that he likes the way the program is structured. He says that he found it easy to follow and liked the use of comments. Again, although not directly relevant, the scribe notes the comment.

The chairman comments on the way the customer details are validated and the fact that two reads on the Customer File are performed where only one is necessary. The programmer comments that she thought her method was safer but is assured it is simply a case of overkill. The scribe notes the change to be made.

Next, the scribe, who is also a programmer, asks if the way the Customer File is indexed could be improved. Blank looks all round, so the chairman puts an action on himself to discuss the matter with the systems programmer and report back.

Finally it is agreed to hold another meeting soon and make the program changes discussed. Program timings are suggested as a way of gauging any improved performance. The meeting closes. A very useful forty-five minutes!

CHAPTER 8
Program maintenance

Ever since the first program was written, there has existed a need for program maintenance. It is generally not viewed as the most exciting of tasks. In any live system support environment, however, there will always be the need for such a task. Sooner or later you will find yourself faced with the task, or opportunity, of maintaining someone else's COBOL program.

After the implementation of any new system, much time will be spent on program maintenance. Why is this and how should the task be approached? Indeed, what is program maintenance?

Program maintenance involves changing an already implemented program, whether running as part of a system or simply a stand-alone program. The magnitude of the problem will range from a few very simple code changes through to an extensive program rewrite – in this case it can be better to completely redesign and write the program from scratch.

Program maintenance will generally be required for one of two reasons. Either errors exist, usually at a coding level but sometimes in the design or more acceptably, enhancements or changes to the program's function are required.

Coding errors will at times not be caught by program testing, especially in the more complex programs written. Thorough testing should detect the vast majority of problems but, as in any new system, bugs or errors will escape the net and not be detected until some period of time has passed – sometimes years! Program design errors, usually introduced at the time of program specification, will not be caught by program testing. Program testing is carried out in part against the specified function of the program. Design errors will not always be apparent to the programmer following a program specification.

Secondly, maintenance will involve program enhancements or functional changes. Such maintenance results not from ordinary coding errors but usually from requests from users for changes, amendments to legislation or system enhancements.

So, program maintenance results from two basic causes:

Program Error – Code or Design.
New Requirements.

It is for these two reasons that we perform program maintenance. Before considering the approach to such a task we should first consider how to code our programs with a view to future maintenance and enhancement.

Coding for future maintenance

By following a few basic guidelines, we can ease the task of support. Program design plays an important part in easing the burden. Structure your programs in a logical and manageable top-down approach by defining functional areas as COBOL Sections. Use comments at the beginning of your program to firstly describe the program function, secondly the program structure in terms of named sections and thirdly provide an outline modification box so that any changes can be documented as part of the source code.

General comments throughout the program and the use of manageable sized sections will ease the time spent in trying to understand the existing code before changing it. The use of departmental programming standards will also provide a common basis on which to begin understanding the program.

Of additional value will be, of course, the provision of concise, complete and up-to-date program documentation. The creation of program documentation is discussed elsewhere in this book.

When first coding with a view to eventual maintenance remember the following:

(1) Structure your program.
(2) Use comments sensibly.
(3) Code an outline Modification box.
(4) Code to existing Programming Standards.
(5) Provide program documentation.

How to approach program maintenance

For any activity to be successful, a well devised plan of attack should be agreed upon. Consider though what maintenance actually involves. When you develop a new program everything is on your side, you have time to set up test data, the chance to properly code your program and only when you are satisfied, deadlines not withstanding, do you implement your program. Maintenance differs in that what you are changing is a live program with an existing user base and user expectations.

To stand a chance of success, a highly achievable goal, the following is a suggested but by no means definitive method.

Program maintenance should be carried out in a controlled manner. Any program changes required should be logged and approved by your manager or team leader before any work begins. This idea is known as 'Change Control'. Change Control controls and supervises program maintenance. It is a simple organisational method to log change requests, initiate the work and approve implementation. If changes were made *ad hoc*, there would be a real lack of method in the maintenance function and worse would follow. It could become common for more than one person to be working on the same program at the same time – a situation not unknown! So before you begin, check that the work has been accepted and scheduled to progress.

When changing any program you should always work on a copy of the source code and not the only live version. It is all too easy to believe that changes made can be reversed by re-editing the code – they cannot! Use standard departmental naming conventions to identify which source is live and which is a test version.

When making changes, document them. Use the modification box at the beginning of the program and include comments, identified by your initials and the date, to annotate your code. Do not forget to increment the program version number so that everyone knows which version is currently running.

Re-testing the program should be mandatory. The existing test plan, filed with the rest of the program documentation, can be used as the basis for creating an additional test plan. Test the program and document the results.

Once everyone is happy with the program and it has been signed off for implementation, actual implementation can take place. Rename your program so that it becomes the live version and the previous live version becomes the back-up. Use standard naming conventions for this – if none exists then make suggestions! Also make the relevant departments aware of the newly implemented changes, whether they be your users, clients or computer operations department. At this point you should also ensure that existing program documentation is kept up to date.

Program maintenance is an important function, especially so because it will often be user departments who have particular expectations riding on the success or failure of your work. Take great care and if in doubt at any time seek guidance from your colleagues or manager. Use the following check points to aid the process.

(1) Work within Change Control procedures.
(2) Work on a copy of the source code.
(3) Annotate changes made.
(4) Re-test the program.
(5) Implement by renaming sources.
(6) Update program documentation.

CHAPTER 9
Documentation

Documentation is an integral part of any system. It applies to many levels of system development and system life. The purpose of such documentation and the area it describes is almost infinite. In whatever form it might take, it is a vital element in the make-up of any system. If you regard the idea of documentation as boring you have already discounted a major part of any element. Many of the chapters discuss techniques or methodologies – they all document in one form or another.

Every system will be described in terms of documentation. Such documents will describe entire systems from a business view whilst others will detail the functions of a specific piece of system software. Such documents may be in the form of prose while others will take the form of annotated diagrams. Documentation has many forms, each specific to the entity being described. Consider for yourself how many different types of documentation you can think of. Potentially, the list should be a large one. You are perhaps most likely to consider documentation in terms of the programs you write e.g. program specifications, and the way in which they are described – a systems analyst might produce a very different list.

When creating documentation consider the potential audience and the area being described. Use an appropriate method whether it is a diagram or text. Finally remember that however good a piece of documentation is, it becomes almost worthless if it is not maintained and is allowed to become out-of-date.

Why document?

As possibly inexperienced programmers, you will be faced with the task of documenting your work. The traditional attitude to documenting is that it is time consuming, unnecessary and liable to become quickly out of date.

Documentation should be written before, during and after the development of any system, whether it is a COBOL program or full application system. The advantages gained include the general control of what is being done and what has been agreed regarding work yet to be done. Clarification exists on work performed which means that there should never be just one centre of knowledge – always an undesirable and dangerous situation to be in. To change any system the current state needs to be known.

Documentation at a system level defines a system for technical staff, analysts as well as users. Remember that such details can range from a functional system overview through to user training and reference guides. Program documentation is likely to be specific to a different type of user – you the programmer.

To summarise so far, we document to provide the following advantages:

(1) Clarification of a current situation.
(2) Help when making changes.
(3) Providing knowledge for specific requirement areas.
(4) Assisting with system maintenance.
(5) Recording work done.

It is hoped that by now you should be able to appreciate the reasons for documenting, at whatever level. As mentioned earlier, you are most likely to be involved with the task of program documentation. If performed properly in a well structured and professional environment it need not be the arduous task it might at first appear.

Program documentation

If you are ever called upon to change an existing program you will form at least two opinions on the documentation provided. Firstly, does it actually exist? Secondly, is the documentation actually up-to-date and of use?

If you are performing maintenance using existing program documentation, then your ability to influence the quality of the articles will be limited to 'change' information. On the other hand a 'green field' situation will allow you the chance to create useful and informative program documentation. Questions to ask yourself include the obvious, 'Do we have existing program documentation standards?'. If the answer is yes then you should follow the standards already installed. Do, however, be ever ready to suggest improvements or additions to existing standards. As a department member your opinion is as important as anyone else's.

What should such documentation consist of?

Beliefs vary but the following can be regarded as a suggested standard.

Documentation is developed in line with the development of the actual program, see Fig. 9.1. Such a situation suggests a natural development path. This will begin with your being given a program specification. Use the specification as your first piece of program documentation – start a folder to hold all the associated documents. Your assimilation of the specification contents will be likely to follow. Any inconsistencies or ambiguities should be

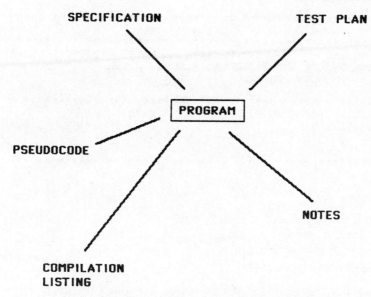

Fig. 9.1 Program documentation

documented as agreed between analyst and programmer.

Designing the actual program can generate a reasonable volume of paper work. Some of this 'paper' will be useful only to yourself and eventually discarded. Of use will be the more formal design tools used such as decision tables, pseudocode and task-specific flowcharts. If considered useful, and legible, these can be included. As you include new items, maintain a basic contents page to be filed in your program folder.

Testing plays a major part in the development of any program. Your test plan and test results should be included once the program has been finished. The advantages are twofold, firstly a test plan and results document the testing of the program and secondly, if changes need to be made the test plan can be used to retest changes made. A natural addition to the documentation will be a program listing – ideally this should be a full compilation listing and not simply a list of the source code.

As changes to the program are made, after the program has been designated 'live', a list of changes should be included on a 'change control' sheet. Any program changes should of course also be reflected in the modification boxes of the actual program itself, see Fig. 9.2.

By the time the program becomes part of a complete application system, a reasonable amount of documentation will have been generated.

To summarise, a folder for each program should contain the following suggested items:

(1) Contents.
(2) Program Specification.

```
****************************************************************
*          C H A N G E     H I S T O R Y                      *
****************************************************************
* MOD: 45              BY: P.SMITH      DATE: 9/9/89          *
* REASON: TO ADD 2 DECIMAL PLACES TO THE                     *
*              COST COLUMN.                                   *
*                                                            *
****************************************************************
* MOD:                 BY:              DATE:                *
* REASON:                                                    *
*                                                            *
*                                                            *
****************************************************************
```

Fig. 9.2

(3) Design material used. e.g. pseudocode.
(4) Program Compilation listing.
(5) Test plan and test results.
(6) Implemented program changes.

A 'contents' page might at first appear obvious or it might seem an unnecessary inclusion. What it does, however, is to describe just what documentation is provided and clarification of what information is present, just in case something has been lost or mislaid.

Including the program specification is easy to do and also very necessary. Whilst the program might have undergone functional changes since its first writing, the specification gives the required background on what the program was originally meant to do. It is also likely to detail files or tables used, validation, processing rules etc. In fact a well written program specification should detail all the required information – if it does not then buy the author a copy of this book, they might benefit.

The program compilation listing is another piece of documentation in its own right. The listing should be a well annotated, well structured piece of code – in fact almost self explanatory. When making changes update a 'modification' box at the beginning of the program and re-compile to generate a new listing. Remember that a simple source program listing will not include any file descriptions, subroutines or modules copied into the program at compile time. Neither will it generate linking information, program warnings or other such cross-referencing information. The inclusion of a listing is very important but does of course introduce the problem of keeping listing and other documentation in an easily managed package.

If testing has been carried out properly then a test plan and completed test results will have been produced. It may at first seem somewhat pedantic to include such material but consider the implications of making a program change. Do you retest the program? Of course you do. The original test plan can often be used as the basis for such testing, saving time and reinvention of the wheel.

In addition to up-dating a program modification box when program changes are made, a more formal method of recording should also be used. Any functional change will affect the way a program works. The date and nature of any such changes should be detailed and included as part of the program documentation. This allows a history of changes to be built up. If there is no managed control over changes, which there really should be, a 'change in progress' chart should also be deployed – two people working on the same program can be very dangerous!

System documentation

System documentation can conjure up many visions. To some it means complex annotated flowcharts, to others it encompasses large volumes of technical description and to others again it may even be represented by a dog-eared collection of faded program listings! At the simplest level system documentation can be thought of as describing a complete application in a technical and non-technical way. How exactly, will vary according to the methods and standards used.

The controlled development of any system creates a series of deliverable documents. These will vary in format according to their intended audience and purpose. The subject is an incredibly wide and diverse one. Take a few minutes to consider what types of material we are talking about when we refer to 'system documentation'. The list is almost endless. Are we considering the subject from an analyst's point of view? Are we using specific charting techniques or design methodologies?

Clearly system documentation can take a variety of possible forms. For the sake of simplicity we will consider the basic items you might expect to come across in a basic system development. Of course different terms are often used to describe the same items in different methodologies but the basic principles remain the same.

Briefly, before we continue, you might be questioning the use of the word 'methodology'. Different companies and organisations standardise on specifically defined approaches to the analysis and design stages of system development. A methodology is a defined set of guidelines, standards etc. created to act as an established framework in which to perform. Often basic deliverables are defined, e.g. a system overview or system diagram. Deliverables are basically the result of a specified project phase, as mentioned above a deliverable could be the completion of a system overview.

The initial components of system documentation will often describe the application in business terms. The idea of using a computer to provide an applications solution will not initially be addressed. Of relevance will be the workings of any existing business system. This will take the form of a general overview describing current working practices or those envisaged. A well structured textual document should result.

Next will follow a document describing the functional aspects of the new system, again in business terms but at a more detailed level. Again, the structure of such a document is exceedingly important. Not only is structure important in terms of general layout, numbering conventions, diagrams etc. but also from the point of view of the actual system being described. Functional areas should be identified and described in an ordered fashion, one function leading to the next with like tasks grouped together. The operation described will of course influence the precise order used.

Numerous charting techniques exist to describe business functions and are described more fully in the next chapter. Activity diagrams are one such standard. These describe parts of an organisation in terms of activities performed, describing the relationships and work cycles involved. Remember that there has not yet been any mention of computer oriented concepts. In days gone by, any system was often designed around the basic concept of files, from the very beginning of the design process. Nowadays the initial limitations of physical computer restraints are ignored – the user requirements take precedence.

The natural progression from functional design will be computer design. This will be described at a number of levels, from basic overview to individual program specifications through to system implementation and production rules. It should be quite obvious that to produce such a document will be no small task, indeed we are probably actually describing a series of related documents.

As before, charting techniques are a vital and invaluable component of system design and specification. Various standards exist, one of the more widely used now being that of 'entity' diagrams. Database systems often use such techniques, describing entities e.g. an invoice, and their relationships between other entities. Entity diagrams are discussed further in the section on charting techniques.

Program specifications make up the third major area of system documentation i.e. the computer solution that will be finally implemented.

Obviously this brief overview cannot fully describe the 'look' of a full set of systems' documentation. The format will vary from one organisation to another. Having a basic appreciation, however, will allow you to understand such documentation better when you no doubt come across it. Expect to see something similar to the following:

(1) System Overview.
(2) Functional system design.
(3) Computer system design.
(4) Program Specifications.

In conclusion, documenting is not considered a particularly exciting activity. It is though very necessary, whether considering a simple program or a complete system. It acts as a record of work done, procedures, relationships, functions, activities – potentially almost everything. To be useful it should be well structured, concise, properly organised, up-to-date and locateable. The need to maintain such a resource must be recognised by all and the rules applied.

The use of such data is changing. With the increased utilisation of such tools as data dictionaries the way information can be stored and retrieved is dramatically influencing the entire way systems are developed. Not only textual but also graphic information can be stored, retrieved, cross-referenced and generally manipulated in a way not as yet known. The advantages are numerous. There becomes a centralised source of information accessible to all where changes are reflected instantly and structure allows infinite views of the data. The data dictionary is a database in its own right, to use it as a documentation tool seems obvious now but has been a long time in coming.

CHAPTER 10

Charting techniques

Charting techniques have in recent years become an integral part of system design. In years gone by the use of such techniques was limited in general to that of program flowcharts and system flowcharts. This has now all changed.

What are charting techniques and what use are they? Basically charting techniques are diagramming standards applied to particular organisation needs. They provide a common visual document that can be created, refined and updated. Such diagrams can be used to describe many different situations at many levels. Examples could include the placing of an order by telephone, detailed by an 'activity diagram'. Alternatively, a complete stock control system might be described using 'entity modelling'.

The worth of such techniques should be obvious. Consider how easy it would be for a system designer to talk you through the basics of a complete system by walking-through an activity diagram with you. Whilst you would not have a complete understanding of the system, you would have gained a reasonably comprehensive overview of events. Compare this idea with that of reading a lengthy system document in an attempt to achieve the same result – not only would it take much more time but would also be a test of stamina too!

Obviously there will always be a need for the written word. In systems however, the use of charting techniques provides a new and valuable angle to that of system documentation, at all levels. The advantages of such diagrams should now be apparent. Consider for yourself the implications.

Before looking at specific approaches we will first consider the advantages in charting and how they can be used at all levels of system building.

Why chart?

Designing anything is never easy. Problems arise for many reasons – the complexity of something, ambiguity, not understanding and so on. Charts and diagrams allow us the opportunity to build a picture of a particular situation. Consider how you design and write a program. You should begin by considering the basic functions from a simplified level and then break down the functions into smaller functional areas – diagrams give you this strength, see Fig. 10.1. 'A Picture paints a thousand words.'

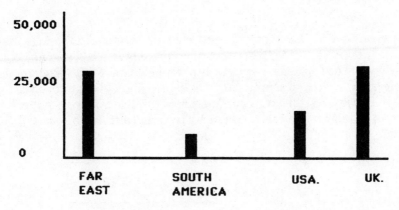

Fig. 10.1 Sales of product X for 1989

Systems can often be badly designed simply because of the approach taken. Diagrams allow a top-down approach to be taken. It can all too easily become overwhelmed at the initial stages. A top-down charting technique allows this problem to be overcome. The idea of 'placing an order' can be represented by just one box on a piece of paper, only later does it need to be further refined.

There is a major advantage at the analysis stage with respect to the user community. Users are generally busy people loath to spend more time than necessary with the analyst, even when it is to their advantage to do so. Users will find diagrams much easier to understand than becoming confused by large volumes of text – diagrams not only show events they can also represent the flow of information.

Types of charts

As we examine the various charting techniques, it will become apparent how many different types of chart can be produced. Obviously different techniques can be used to represent different situations and applications. Not only should the specific situation be considered but also the end-user, use of the chart, drawing method etc.

Some charts need to show the flow of information whilst others do not. The display of decisions can be important in some cases, elsewhere decisions will not be shown. The relationships between data items will on occasions be significant and so on. The objective of the chart, the process it is trying to reflect and the way in which it will be used is of significant importance – that is why so many different charting techniques exist, being grouped into a number of forms to suit the situation.

Flowcharts

These were one of the earliest charting techniques devised. The basic concept was to produce a start to finish series of events, represented by a number of different shaped boxes – very much a 'straight line form' diagram. To navigate the chart you simply started at the top and walked through to the finish. Flowcharts still have some limited value but are difficult to use, it is not easy to jump into the middle of such a chart and attempt to learn its logic, see Fig. 10.2.

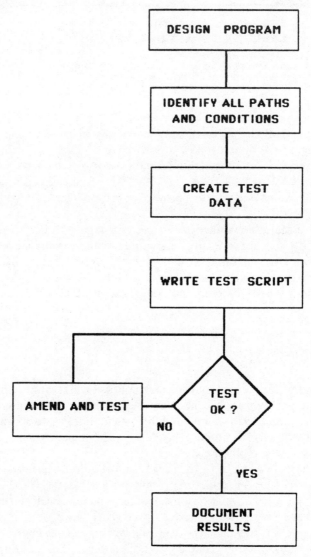

Fig. 10.2 Program testing

Tree structures

Such charts can take one of two basic forms; either a binary tree or an open-tree structure. Tree structures can be employed to show hierarchical patterns. From the parent node of a tree children can branch off in a downward direction.

In a binary tree there can only be two children to each parent, in other trees there can be many children to each adult. Tree diagrams lend themselves well to the hierarchical situation and also to the 'yes–no' decision type application. A binary tree can be used to describe a condition with each branch representing 'yes' and 'no' respectively.

Such charts are often drawn in a top-to-bottom, left-to-right approach. They can also be drawn, however, on their side. Such diagrams can be difficult to update once drawn and can become quite large. Showing a sequence can sometimes be a problem though it is generally well implied. It is worth noting that some database systems rely on a hierarchical approach and use such diagrams to define particular data structures, see Fig. 10.3. Databases are described later in this book.

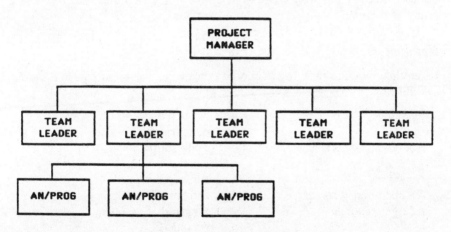

Fig. 10.3 A hierarchical structure

Data model diagrams

This is one of the fastest growing charting techniques employing a diversity of methods and techniques. The subject of data model diagrams is a wide one. The diversity of such charts is wide – some diagrams show quite explicitly the flow of data while others concentrate on the relationships between particular data items or describe specific processes and actions.

Examples of data model diagrams include DFD or data flow diagrams and entity–relationship diagrams. Both methods are described in more detail next.

Four charting methods

As can be seen, many considerations go into choosing a particular charting method. To use such methods we need to consider in a little more detail the application, notation etc. of such methods.

Let us now look, in a little more detail, at some specific methods currently in use:

(1) Activity diagrams.
(2) Data flow diagrams.
(3) Entity–relationship diagrams.
(4) Action diagrams.

Activity diagrams

Such diagrams are best used at the analysis stage of a project. The basic idea is to produce one or more diagrams that detail the functional aspects of an existing or proposed system.

When creating any system, the basis should not be how the computer can be designed to handle the job but what are the features required at a business level – activity diagrams serve to document this.

Notation

Like other standard charting methods, a particular symbol notation is used as follows:

Rectangle	=	An activity e.g. generate invoice
Round-ended rectangle	=	Data source e.g. a user
An arrow	=	Flow
An open-ended rectangle	=	Information store
A large rectangle	=	A group of associated activities – bounded

Some definitions

- Activity – basically acts upon input information to generate some form of output information.
- Data source – a source of information such as a customer.
- Information store – stored information such as customer addresses or a set of rules.

Use

As mentioned earlier, such diagrams depict the general flow of information

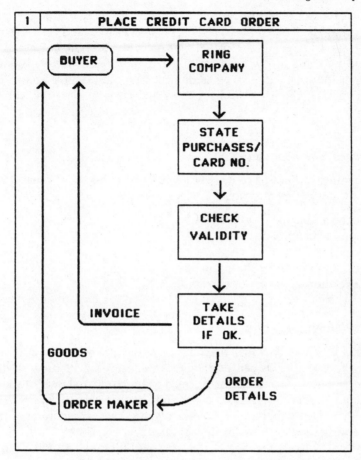

Fig. 10.4 Placing a credit card order – activity diagram

through a number of activities. Consider any business function that you are reasonably familiar with and try to define the different activities and pieces of information involved. An example might be placing a telephone order using a credit card – an activity diagram could easily reflect this process, see Fig. 10.4.

As the example shows, the customer is shown as a data source. The invoice is shown as an information store and the taking of the order as an activity. Arrows show the actual flow of the process.

By simply picking up this chart and possessing only a basic knowledge of the notation used, it would quickly be possible to determine the actions involved within the process. Indeed, it would not be difficult to 'walk through' the chart with a user to confirm or clarify the situation. By building up a series of charts using a top-down approach, it becomes reasonably easy to define a complete system at a functional level in an easily accepted form.

Once the fundamental principles have been understood, the annotational rules can be applied. Apart from labelling the overall chart and various boxes of equal importance are the data flows shown. These flows should be annotated by using arrow heads at either or both ends and in addition labelling the flow e.g. 'authorised credit order' on our example above. The overall idea is to eliminate any ambiguity and create a clear and concise diagram.

Advantages and disadvantages

Such diagrams will not of course always be appropriate but do have their place in the development process.

(1) Describe a functional system clearly.
(2) A top-down approach can be used.
(3) Standard notation used.
(4) Tends not to consider the computer.
(5) Data relationships are not apparent.

Data flow diagrams

The idea of DFDs or data flow diagrams takes the idea of activity diagrams one stage further. DFDs can be thought of as showing the flow of data through a system. The processes performed on the data are shown, as well as sources and destinations. Various boxes and lines are used to define such a picture. It is in DFDs that the idea of an arrow becomes especially important – arrows being used to show the flow of data.

The system analysis stage will be the area that DFDs are most likely to be applied to. The flow of data can be described at a logical level with no need to consider the specific physical organisation of the data to be handled. As with activity diagrams, a top-down approach can be taken with individual processes being identified and further decomposed.

DFDs are becoming one of the more widely used analysis tools used in many of the larger organisations. The time spent invested at this stage will reap benefits in the later system creation activities.

Notation

As with any other method specific symbols have specific meanings. DFDs use just four symbols:

A square	=	Data source or destination
A rounded rectangle	=	A process
Open-ended rectangle	=	A store of data
An arrow	=	Flow of data

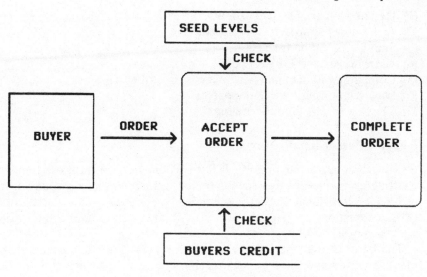

Fig. 10.5 Plant seed order – DFD

Some definitions

- Data source/destination – any originator or holder of data. Often a person e.g. an accountant.
- A process – any procedure that changes the flow of data.

Look at the example in Fig. 10.5 using the DFD notation as a key. Try to follow the flow of data or information through this subsystem. This could be just one part of a large system and you should be able to see how the top-down approach can again be taken. Instead of the process boxes detailing specific actions, another overview DFD could have a process box annotated 'order seeds' – the example above would be a decomposition of that.

The strength of such a technique should be obvious from an analytical point of view. But how would the knowledge of such a technique benefit you as a programmer? When doing part of any job it always helps to be aware of the total picture even if only from a limited viewpoint. By recognising the total picture you are better able to spot deficiencies and ambiguities as well as approach maintenance and enhancements from a more enlightened point of view. It will make the task more interesting if you can see where the results of your efforts will fit in.

If your organisation uses DFDs, take the opportunity to study them and ask questions – understanding the total system picture will make you a known and valuable member of the team.

Advantages and disadvantages

DFDs can be a useful technique. Consider the following:

(1) Describe a logical system clearly.
(2) A top-down approach can be used.
(3) Standard notation used.
(4) Users understand DFDs.
(5) Computer and manual systems can be described.
(6) Data relationships are not apparent.
(7) The task can be time consuming.

Entity–relationship diagrams

Entity–relationship diagramming is fast becoming one of the most popular charting techniques, further fuelled by the upsurge in the use of database techniques. Relational database systems lend themselves quite well to the use of entity–relationship diagrams and the two are often used in conjunction with each other.

The basic concept behind such diagrams is, as the name suggests, to identify entities and show the relationship types amongst such entities. As with other methods, the usual top-down approach can be taken. Charts can be created showing as much or little detail as required. These entity–relationship diagrams can later be decomposed also into detailed data models.

By working closely with user departments it is possible for the analyst to create a detailed entity–relationship diagram that models an entire organisation's data.

Notation

At the topmost level there are only two basic symbols.

A rectangle	=	An entity
An arrow	=	The relationship

Some definitions

Basically something about which we can store data. e.g. a customer, a bank account.

A relationship describes the association between two entities. A number of relationship types exist.

Different relationships – there are generally recognised as being three basic relationship types:

- One-to-one – entity A is associated with just one of entity B. Shown by a straight line.
- One-to-many – entity A is associated with one or more of entity B. Shown as a line with one crow's foot.
- Many-to-many – many entity A are associated with many B. Shown as a line with a crow's foot at either end. Note that many-to-many relationships are discouraged because of their complexity, see Fig. 10.6.

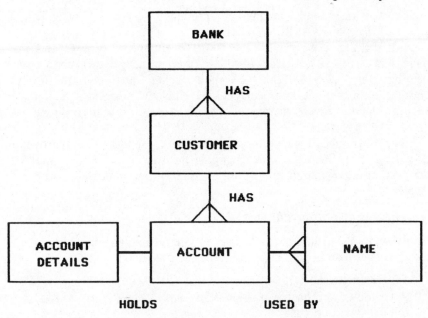

Fig. 10.6 Entity-relationship diagram showing a simplified bank model

The notation used in entity–relationship diagrams can be more involved that other conventions. This idea is carried on through into the way diagrams are annotated. Opinions differ on this subject but the following is a suggested convention.

Designers often try to make their charts read like sentences. So they might have:

i.e. 'a customer account contains one or more transaction entries.'

This is the basic charting notation. In addition there are further relationship types to describe mutual exclusion, zero or one etc.

The example details a very simple entity–relationship model of a bank. Each bank has zero, one or more customers. Each customer can have one or more accounts with each account having one or more names attached to it, e.g. husband and and wife. In addition, every account has a set of account details i.e. overdraft limit, address etc.

Such diagrams show entities and their relationships. These diagrams can be further refined to produce detailed data models. Even at a simple level this principle can be applied. So an entity can be of a particular entity type with various attributes. These attributes can have values that can be grouped together – records can be mapped onto entities.

So, a customer entity might be represented by the following fields: CUSTOMER NO, NAME, ADDRESS.

With the increasing developments in development software and the increasing complexity of charts produced, there seems a natural connection between the two. Systems are now being developed to design entity–relationship models while concurrently creating data dictionary entries. Amendments to the model are reflected elsewhere accordingly – a powerful tool.

Powerful graphics workstations are required for this task but the hardware does now exist. Such tools are changing the role of the system analyst, designer, database administrator and of course programmer.

Advantages and disadvantages

Entity–relationship diagrams are a fast growing technique. Like every system they have good and bad points. Consider the following:

(1) Describe a logical system clearly.
(2) A top-down approach can be used.
(3) Standard notation used.
(4) Data can be clearly described.
(5) Users understand simple charts.
(6) New technology supports this method.
(7) Data relationships are apparent.
(8) Diagrams can become complex.
(9) Not a traditional approach.

Action diagrams

We have so far considered three charting techniques: activity diagrams, data flow diagrams, entity–relationship diagrams. Each of these approaches takes the analysis–design stage one stage further, without taking into account the separate task of program building.

Action diagrams are in many ways similar to the box-and-line program design approach. What differs is the actual notation used and more dramatically, the use of lines but no boxes!

Cast your mind back to the description of program design using box-and-line charts. The basic idea was to take a top-down approach by defining overall functional areas and breaking them down into program sections. These sections could then be sequenced into logical groupings and individually coded. Action diagrams take a similar approach.

Notation

Instead of using a box to represent a module or section a bracket is drawn.

A bracket   =   A program section

This really is the basis of the method. Brackets are used in a vertical line to show different processes.

A process might be to calculate an invoice total and print the results. As with all methods, additional annotation puts detail on the basic notation – some examples will be given of this, see Fig. 10.7.

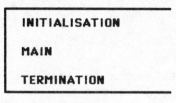

INITIALISATION

MAIN

TERMINATION

Fig. 10.7

This very basic action diagram describes the overall structure of any COBOL program.

A more complicated example might take the form shown in Fig. 10.8.

Note the double horizontal lines at the top of the diagram, these indicate repetition of the process.

The previous example shows no specific condition handling. Conditions are handled in the way shown in Fig. 10.9.

Note that the dividing line between the two possible answers denotes mutual exclusion i.e. the condition can be true or false.

From the above examples it can be seen how a simple overall structure can be decomposed into greater levels of detail. Coding from such a design

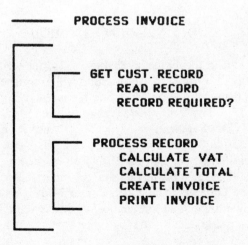

PROCESS INVOICE

GET CUST. RECORD
READ RECORD
RECORD REQUIRED?

PROCESS RECORD
CALCULATE VAT
CALCULATE TOTAL
CREATE INVOICE
PRINT INVOICE

Fig. 10.8

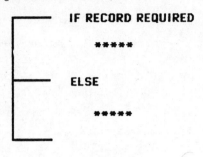

IF RECORD REQUIRED

*****

ELSE

*****

Fig. 10.9

should not be an overly complex task. As with all charting techniques the diagram acts as excellent documentation.

Additional notations include the use of Case Structures, Nesting, Do While etc. – all common processing forms. Indeed you should be able to see a connection between action diagrams and pseudocode; the two are not that far removed.

Action diagrams provide a useful program design methodology. Whilst not being the ultimate design tool there is definite value in its application. The use of brackets and incrementation impose a natural use of programming standards.

Advantages and disadvantages

(1) A top-down approach can be used.
(2) Easy to create.
(3) Help create good programming standards.
(4) Not the most sophisticated design tool.

What makes a good charting technique?

There are many charting techniques available for use, but what makes a good method. Obviously the answer to this question will to some extent be based on either personal preference or what one has been used to using – the department standard can often influence the response.

Sometimes the type of application used will influence the method used or the file organisation or software e.g. database. Perhaps the programming language or overall methodology used has an influence. Whatever the reasons however, there remains the fact that the method used is either good or bad. How do we judge whether a particular method is good or not? Again this will come down to personal preference to some extent. There do exist, however, specific criteria that we can use when trying to reach an answer.

(1) The chart should be easy to design and read.

(2) The notation used should not be over complex.
(3) Functions and data should be catered for.
(4) The method should lend itself to a structured top-down approach.
(5) The file organisation should be taken into consideration but not restrained by physical detail.
(6) Automated system generation should be feasible.

The changing face of charting techniques

As already mentioned, the techniques employed when charting have changed considerably over the last ten years. The most common method was that of the flowchart, as either a program flowchart or system flowchart.

Program flowcharts described a series of actions and decisions. Such decisions could result in being either true or false with symbols to represent the different step types. The result would usually be a long and difficult to follow line of symbols – not always useful and generally difficult to maintain.

System flowcharts also used a number of different charting symbols to represent entity types such as a 'program', 'disk' or 'sorting process'. Because of the symbol meanings, there was a strong tendency to design physical computer systems from the beginning. It was easy to become embroiled in the basic computer concepts of disk files, printed reports etc. Such charts can still prove useful but only to document an already designed system, not as part of the functional design. The emphasis is now on the functional design of the system, initially ignoring physical constraints.

In the mid to late seventies the approach to charting changed. New structured design methodologies began to be introduced. With such methods came new and revolutionary charting techniques. The need for standardised and methodical approaches to analysis and design meant that new methods were soon adopted. With the further developments of database systems and the decreasing use of traditional batch systems such procedures became even more important and much more relevant.

The early eighties has seen the increased use of specific database organisations. New charting methods have evolved to cope with these innovative systems. More recently, the use of automated design aids has given even greater power to the system designer. Graphics workstations and sophisticated plotters allow systems to be drawn and redrawn before ever putting pen to paper. Indeed, it is now possible to 'chart' a system and then automatically generate code to produce the system!

CAD (computer aided design) is changing the way systems are designed, but again they rely on the basic rules of standardisation. It is also true that the 'garbage-in, garbage-out' rule still applies. There will always be the need for human input, these systems merely ease the process of creating ever more complex systems.

Such computer design systems can be incredibly powerful tools. It is possible to create designs and then use the computer to verify such systems for consistency across entity types. When changing relationships between entities, other related entities can be automatically updated or inconsistencies highlighted. There is also the obvious added advantage that different designs can be 'road-tested' before implementation and the visual results talked through with the more astute users.

Finally, such methods suggest the use of data dictionaries as a natural addition to the documentation armoury. With huge amounts of background data being collated, data dictionaries are the ideal way of holding and maintaining the 'data behind the symbol'.

We have looked at the basic idea behind charting techniques, a few simple chart types and the way the science has changed over the years. So what are the advantages of such techniques?

Summary

We have considered a number of aspects on charting techniques. We have considered why they are actually used and the different types of chart in use.

The methods and techniques employed over the years have been refined. No longer are program and system flowcharts the only diagrams created. Indeed the traditional program flowchart has quite rightly gone out of fashion and been superseded by the introduction of programming standards, structured methods and fourth generation languages.

With the development of powerful workstations and new design software, charts can be designed, drawn and modified many times before ever reaching a piece of paper. Data dictionaries can be linked with such applications to further standardise the task.

We have briefly looked at four different charting techniques: activity diagrams, data flow diagrams, entity–relationship diagrams and action diagrams. Each has its own part to play and individual area of interest. Not all these methods will be used in every organisation. The strength of such methods is to standardise on one or two particular ones, appropriate to the organisation. Standardisation is the key, it creates a common language constrained in the best possible way by a formal and structured framework.

So why use charting techniques?

(1) A sense of standardisation is introduced.
(2) An excellent design tool.
(3) Structured methods become mandatory.
(4) Change becomes easy.
(5) A documentation aid.
(6) Automated design methods can be used.

PART 2

Practical examples

Part 2 outlines four different case examples of program development. Each case, using COBOL and SQL, examines a different type of program as well as various programming implications.

The SQL statements are embedded into standard COBOL. Note that the implementation shown may well differ from that on other machines but the basic principles remain the same.

CHAPTER 11

The development of a batch COBOL/SQL system

This first case will look at the development of one program within a suite of programs. The application will be based on relational database concepts using a mixture of COBOL and SQL (Structured Query Language).

To understand the way we will use and mix database and standard COBOL statements together, it is worth spending a short time describing the concepts behind the most popular and fast developing relational database technology. We will then go on to develop a COBOL/SQL database program.

Relational database systems overview

Relational database systems are becoming one of the most popular of database structures. Many of the larger software developers are now taking the relational path, developing integrated relational systems. Such systems can now be bought comprising the actual database system, data dictionaries, screen painters and report generators – all as a complete integrated system. Supported by strong advertising, the relational market has become a very large one.

The fundamental principles behind relational databases rely on the idea of tables. Tables are collections of organised data where each table can map onto an entity on an entity diagram.

The following example shows a simple table used in a 'customer booking

CUSTOMER

CUST_NO	NAME	ADDRESS
3452	B.SMITH	18, THE GROVE
1890	L.G.BROWN	341, THE ROAD
1886	B.DATE	26, RIPON WAY
2310	F.WHITE	23B, THE FLAT
6664	S.D.ROBIN	28, THE LANE

Fig. 11.1

system', the customer table is shown in Fig. 11.1.

It should be noted that each row represents a record while each column represents an attribute. In relational terminology, a table is called a relation, rows are sometimes known as tuples and columns as attributes – these terms can be confused however and are not commonly used in industry.

The use of tables is fundamental but the idea goes beyond the simple table idea – a series of rules must also be adhered to:

(1) Columns all contain the same category of value.
(2) Each column has a unique name.
(3) Each row is unique.
(4) The ordering of rows and columns is not significant.
(5) Where a column/row has no value, it is known as having a null value.

We have so far just looked at the way one table can be constructed. You are probably thinking that it looks just like a file that could be accessed and indexed sequentially via a COBOL program. In many ways you would be absolutely correct, the strength of relational databases only becomes apparent when you have a number of related tables. With a group of tables all adhering to the relational rules, many powerful operations can be performed on them.

One of the industry terms is SQL (pronounced Sequel). SQL stands for Standard Query Language and forms the basis for a language with which to manipulate a relational database. This particular Data Manipulation Language (DML), is fast becoming a standard, allowing users to access and manipulate a database. Additionally, SQL statements can be embedded into conventional programming languages such as COBOL – more of this later.

To further illustrate the use of this we now need another table. So in addition to Fig. 11.2 we have Fig. 11.3.

We can perform a series of different queries on these two particular tables.

We could, for example, extract all details from the customer table for a particular CUST_NO. Alternatively, we could amend the time of the BC 43 flight to New York knowing that all customer/flight details would automatically reflect the new flight time. If you study the two tables however, you will see that there is no direct link between the two. A third table is

CUSTOMER

CUST_NO	NAME	ADDRESS
3452	B.SMITH	18, THE GROVE
1890	L.G.BROWN	341, THE ROAD
1886	B.DATE	26, RIPON WAY
2310	F.WHITE	23B, THE FLAT
6664	S.D.ROBIN	28, THE LANE

Fig. 11.2

FLIGHTS

FLIGHT_NO	DESTINATION	DATE	TIME
BC 34	LOS ANGELES	11.10.88	11:10
BC 43	NEW YORK	03.09.88	19:30
SI 123	SINGAPORE	26.09.88	09:50
PO 26	WARSAW	25.09.88	13:20

Fig. 11.3

required to create the relationships, more of this soon.

Finally, an overview of relational database systems would not be complete without mentioning normalisation. Although normalisation lies outside the scope of this book, the essential points are discussed below.

Third normal form, often referred to as 3NF, is the normal goal for any database designer. Third normal form is an additional aid in the task of relational database design. Normalisation consists of satisfying a basic set of rules to produce a sound data model. A table is in 3NF if:

(1) There is a unique key for each row. The key may be one or more of the columns in the row.
(2) No duplication of columns or repeating entries.
(3) Columns are mutually independent.
(4) All non-key fields are directly dependent on the whole of the key.

So, to demonstrate normalisation using our customer/flight example. Our customer/flight row could initially have looked like Fig. 11.4.

CUSTOMER/FLIGHT

CUST_NO	NAME	ADDRESS	FLIGHT_NO	DEST.	ETC
3452	SMITH	44	BC 56	HK	
3452	SMITH	44	SI 456	SI	

Fig. 11.4

This can be broken down into first normal form (1NF) to give Fig. 11.5.

Second normal form (2NF) requires that every non-key column is fully dependent on the primary key.

In the example above, both name and address are dependent on the CUST_NO, but the FLIGHT_NO cannot be derived from the CUST_NO, so we have Fig. 11.6.

CUSTOMER

CUST_NO	NAME	ADDRESS	FLIGHT_NO
3452	SMITH	44	BC 56
3452	SMITH	44	SI 456

FLIGHT

FLIGHT_NO	DEST.
BC 56	HK
SI 456	SI

Fig. 11.5

CUSTOMER

CUST_NO	NAME	ADDRESS
3452	SMITH	44
3452	SMITH	44

FLIGHT

FLIGHT_NO	DEST.
BC 56	HK
SI 456	SI

Fig. 11.6

BOOKING

FLIGHT_NO	CUST_NO
BC 56	3452
SI 456	3452

CUSTOMER

CUST_NO	NAME	ADDRESS
3452	SMITH	44
3452	SMITH	44

FLIGHT

FLIGHT_NO	DEST.
BC 56	HK
SI 456	SI

Fig. 11.7

Creating the relationship between the two tables requires a third relation as in Fig. 11.7.

The tables are now in third normal form (3NF).

To briefly summarise, relational database systems are very much the growing database technology. They rely on the principles of entity, attribute, relationship, mapped onto tables and columns. Such database systems provide flexibility and power, now being available in fully integrated database management systems.

Database manipulation

Two main areas exist in manipulating a database; setting up the database tables and actually using it. The DML (Data Manipulation Language), in this case SQL, can either be used on its own or embedded into a particular programming language. COBOL is a very widely used programming language and has an important part to play when interfaced with a DML.

To briefly summarise, there are two basic operations; setting up the database and manipulating the database – either using a direct DML or embedded statements.

Setting up the database

To illustrate this stage we will take the customer/flight example.

SQL allows the user to create a database, interrogate it, update, amend, delete and report on the results. Note that the examples shown are based on a particular implementation of SQL, though any differences should be marginal.

So, to firstly address the question of creating our database we should consider the basic steps involved. The first task would be to analyse requirements and data and then design our entity–relationship diagram. From the entity–relationship diagram we would be able to map our entities to tables. With the aid of data analysis we would also be able to define individual tables attributes, or columns.

Let us use the initial flight/customer example. This would be represented by the entity–relationship diagram in Fig. 11.8.

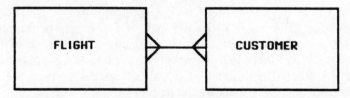

Fig. 11.8 Flights and customers – a many-to-many relationship

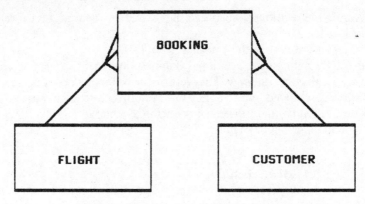

Fig. 11.9 The booking system data diagram

This describes two basic entities; flights and customers to handle a flight booking system at the very simplest level. The diagramming conventions used show a 'double crow's foot'. This indicates a many-to-many relationship, i.e., a flight can have one or more customers and a customer can book one or many flights.

There is some academic argument as to whether many-to-many relationships are valid. They can certainly be inefficient in terms of data duplication and processing. To circumvent this we can introduce a new entity or table, called booking, while still maintaining an implied many-to-many relationship. The value of this should become apparent in the SQL examples.

So our revised entity–relationship diagram would look as in Fig. 11.9.

The new entity, booking, is now included.

So, to create the tables CUSTOMER and FLIGHT as per the previous table diagrams we would use the SQL in Fig. 11.10.

```
CUSTOMER.

CREATE TABLE CUSTOMER
     ( CUST_NO    NUMBER( 4 ) NOT NULL,
       NAME       CHAR( 20 ),
       ADDRESS    CHAR( 40 ) )
```

Fig. 11.10

The above SQL is not COBOL. It would normaly only be performed once by some sort of system administrator or database administrator (DBA). What actually happens is that an empty table structure is created and an area of disk space would be allocated for the table. Once this has been done, rows of data can be inserted, updated and deleted.

The empty structure looks as in Fig. 11.11.

CUSTOMER

CUST_NO	NAME	ADDRESS

Fig. 11.11

FLIGHT.

```
CREATE TABLE FLIGHT
    ( FLIGHT_NO     CHAR(5) NOT NULL,
      DESTINATION   CHAR(15),
      FDATE         DATE,
      FTIME         CHAR(5))
```

Creates an empty structure as in Fig. 11.12.

FLIGHT_NO	DESTINATION	DATE	TIME

Fig. 11.12

FLIGHT_NO	CUST_NO	HOTEL

Fig. 11.13

To create the new bookings table in the form shown in Fig. 11.13.
We would use

BOOKING.

```
CREATE TABLE BOOKING
     ( FLIGHT_NO     CHAR(5) NOT NULL,
       CUST_NO       NUMBER(4),
       HOTEL         CHAR(15))
```

A few words of explanation are useful here. When defining columns they can be defined as a number of different types including CHARacter and NUMBER, the length also needs to be stated. NOT NULL simply means that for that particular column, when a row entry is made the field must be given a value, i.e., it cannot be null, blank, etc.

The three empty tables; flight, booking and customer now exist. By examining the revised entity–relationship diagram, it can be read that for each customer there can be one or more bookings, for each flight there can be one or more bookings.

In business terms we will want to perform many different operations. Consider what they could be. The type of operation will form into one of two basic categories, either amending the tables in some way or viewing the table information. Amending the tables could take the form of making a booking. View table information could, for example, mean reporting on all customers booking on a particular flight. An example is now given.

Check the existence of a flight.
Using SQL we could say:

```
SELECT FLIGHT_NO, DESTINATION, FDATE, FTIME
    FROM FLIGHT
        WHERE DESTINATION = 'SINGAPORE'
```

The basic syntax of this line of SQL is:
    SELECT columns FROM table WHERE condition.
    Alternatively, we could select everything from the Flights table by saying:

```
SELECT * FROM FLIGHT
```

The '*' means all columns. As there is no WHERE condition every row would be selected, i.e., the entire table.

As you can see it is very easy to select from a particular table once the tables exist and contain information. Although such SQL statements can become exceedingly involved and complex, it is still easy to create commanding selection statements in just a couple of lines.

So far we have been selecting from empty tables. Entering data can be performed in a variety of ways. One of the simplest forms is as follows:

```
INSERT INTO CUSTOMER
    VALUES ('2144','MR.SMITH','45 THE LANE')
```

Note that as CUST_NO was specified as NOT NULL it must be given a value, other fields could be left empty. Values used, delimited by commas, are inserted in order into a row in the table named, i.e. CUSTOMER.

So let us assume that all three tables have now been loaded with data giving us the example shown in Fig. 11.14.

FLIGHTS

Key Field

FLIGHT_NO	DESTINATION	DATE	TIME
BA 45	SINGAPORE	12-SEP-88	11:50
SI 12	HONG KONG	23-OCT-88	05:30
SI 67	NEW YORK	14-OCT-88	14:30
PA 90	ROME	06-JAN-89	12:00

CUSTOMER

Key Field

CUST_NO	NAME	ADDRESS
2345	A. JONES	34,RIPON WAY
2120	M.R.JAMES	THE LODGE
1995	M.GREEN	FLAT A
3400	S.LOCK	19, CULDESAC

BOOKING

Key FLIGHT_NO	Field CUST_NO	HOTEL
BA 45	2120	OLAHA
PA 90		OLD TAR
BA 45	2345	OLAHA
BA45	1995	
SI 12	3400	SEAVIEW
SI 67	3400	BIDAWEE

Fig. 11.14

With the tables containing data, we could perform a variety of different queries using the SELECT statement in SQL.

Selecting destinations and dates from the FLIGHTS table

```
SELECT DEST, FDATE FROM FLIGHT
```

would give:

```
SINGAPORE       12-SEP-88
HONG KONG       23-OCT-88
NEW YORK        14-OCT-88
ROME            06-JAN-89
```

Selecting all customer names from the CUSTOMER table

```
SELECT NAME FROM CUSTOMER
```

would give:

```
A.JONES
M.R.JAMES
M.GREEN
S.LOCK
```

A more sophisticated query, using two tables, to select customer details for customers booked on flight BA45

```
SELECT CUSTOMERS.CUST_NO,NAME
    FROM CUSTOMER, BOOKING
WHERE BOOKING.CUST_NO = CUSTOMER.CUST_NO
    AND BOOKING.FLIGHT_NO = 'BA 45'
```

would give

```
2345    A.JONES
2120    M.R.JAMES
1995    M.GREEN
```

This more complex SELECT requires some explanation. Although reasonably simple, the query shows the power available in relational databases and the ease with which they may be queried.

If you look carefully at the statement above you should see that it actually uses two tables, this is the power of relational databases. The FROM line defines the two tables used, i.e., CUSTOMER and BOOKING. As we are using more than one table we can no longer assume that column names are unique, it is for this reason that the column to be selected is prefixed by the table name as: CUSTOMER.CUST_NO,NAME. The final WHERE clause in the select statement again emphasises the power of relational databases, by specifying more than one condition across more than one table.

More SQL examples (try to work out their functions)

It is perhaps worth reiterating that the SQL statements below could be typed in by a programmer at the standard SQL prompt. The statement would execute immediately and the values returned would be displayed on the user's screen,

```
SQL>
SQL> SELECT NAME FROM CUSTOMER WHERE CUST_NO = 3400

    CUSTOMER
    --------
    S.LOCK

    1    rows returned.
SQL>
SQL> SELECT etc, and so on......
```

This method is fine for program development or support work. However, to control the use of such SQL statements, users are normally only given indirect access to the system via menu driven systems and reports with embedded SQL statements. It is very rare for users to be allowed to execute their own SQL statements directly.

```
SELECT CUST_NO,NAME
    FROM CUSTOMER
    ORDER BY NAME


SELECT CUST_NO
    FROM CUSTOMER
    WHERE CUST_NO BETWEEN 500 AND 1200


UPDATE ORDER
    SET ORDER_VALUE = 2134, ITEM_NO = 5
    WHERE ORDER_NO = 54327


DELETE FROM CUSTOMER
    WHERE EMPLOYEE_NO = 5643
```

NULL

NULL values have already been briefly mentioned. They are, however, an important and necessary part of relational database manipulation.

Character NULL values are normally shown as spaces while NULL numeric values are shown as zeroes. It will often occur that a particular field has no value assigned, this is known as a NULL value.

If you refer back to the section on creating table structure you will see that fields could be defined as either NULL or NOT NULL. By specifying NOT NULL it means that the field must always contain a value. When defined as NULL, it is acceptable to leave the field blank.

So, for example, to search an employee table for all those employees who did not receive a discretionary bonus, it would be possible to say:

```
SELECT EMPLOYEE_NO, EMPLOYEE_NAME
    FROM EMPLOYEE
    WHERE BONUS IS NULL
```

i.e., all employees with no entry in their bonus field.

It is also permissible to search using 'IS NOT NULL'.

Sub-queries

Before leaving the specifics of SQL it is certainly worth mentioning the idea of sub-queries. Those who like the concept of nesting will see the power of sub-queries straightaway. Those not so keen on nesting will perhaps need more time to appreciate this powerful concept!

An example will best serve our purposes in describing such queries. When studying the example, consider how much easier it is to follow by using indentation!

```
SELECT EMPLOYEE_NO, EMPLOYEE_NAME
    FROM EMPLOYEE
    WHERE JOB_TYPE =
        ( SELECT JOB_TYPE
          FROM CAREER
          WHERE SALARY_LIMIT > 15000 )
```

By using indentation it is reasonably simple to decipher this example. Consider the innermost query first, which will create a temporary table. The outer query then selects from this table. Sub-queries can become very involved and difficult to maintain. The mandatory use of brackets, however, will help.

Data manipulation using COBOL

From the few brief examples shown above, it can be seen how data can be manipulated using SQL in a relational database environment. You may now be asking yourself what relevance this all has to the use of COBOL. As already mentioned, the increasing use of database systems and fourth-generation languages has increased rapidly in the last few years. COBOL continues to be a driving force in commercial programming but its application is ever changing. These changes involve the use of new data storage techniques – specifically relational databases.

The strength of COBOL relies on its ability to manipulate data and less so on its expertise in accessing it. Many languages now handle indexed as well as sequential processing. COBOL's continued strength lies in its flexible reaction to change, specifically in its ability to include embedded database manipulation statements. The obvious advantage is that skilled COBOL programmers can further develop their existing skills without having to learn completely new ones.

Commit and rollback

Finally, it is worth mentioning the ideas of commit and rollback.

In conventional programming once a record is updated the transaction is completed and the state of the file or files altered. The way to reverse the situation is restore a previous file version or attempt to 'reverse' all the transactions. Many of the more sophisticated database systems support software that can reverse such transactional changes or confirm them.

When changes are committed using a COMMIT statement, all changes to the database are confirmed and cannot be reversed automatically. Before the commit point is reached, it would be possible to reverse or ROLLBACK any changes made, to the previous commit point.

To make this possible special background files are maintained that record any changes made during non-committed phases so that they may be reversed later. Once changes have been committed they cannot be rolled back.

Although not a feature always widely used, it can be very powerful in certain situations and is a powerful feature of several database systems.

We will now look at an example program development using both SQL and COBOL combined. The example takes a Customer Flight booking system as its basis.

System overview

This system is used to record and report on customer made bookings for many available flights. A database is used to record all the information.

This particular program is used to report on customers booked onto a specified flight number.

Program specification

PROGRAM SPECIFICATION.

FL01.

ABC AIRWAYS PLC.

Contents

(1) Contents
(2) Introduction
(3) System flowchart
(4) Input
(5) Output
(6) Processing
(7) Appendix

Introduction

FL01 forms part of the Flight Booking System. Its function is to list all customers booked onto a flight as specified by the user supplied flight number parameter.

A report is produced in printed form detailing flight/customer details. All data are accessed from the Flight database.

System flowchart

See Fig. 11.15.

Fig. 11.15

Input–Output

FLIGHTS database.
Tables: BOOKING, CUSTOMER

BOOKING

Key FLIGHT_NO	Field CUST_NO	HOTEL

CUSTOMER

Key Field CUST_NO	NAME	ADDRESS

Fig. 11.16

Report layout

See Fig. 11.17.

```
SYSTEM XXXXXXXX                                        PAGE 999
DATE 99-99-99          FLIGHTS/CUSTOMERS REPORT
                          FOR FLIGHT XXXXXX
                       ------------------------

CUST NO.    NAME.            ADDRESS.

9999999    XXXXXXXXXXX    XXXXXXXXXXXXXXXXXXXXXXXXXXXXXXXX
9999999    XXXXXXXXXXX    XXXXXXXXXXXXXXXXXXXXXXXXXXXXXXXX
9999999    XXXXXXXXXXX    XXXXXXXXXXXXXXXXXXXXXXXXXXXXXXXX
9999999    XXXXXXXXXXX    XXXXXXXXXXXXXXXXXXXXXXXXXXXXXXXX
9999999    XXXXXXXXXXX    XXXXXXXXXXXXXXXXXXXXXXXXXXXXXXXX
9999999    XXXXXXXXXXX    XXXXXXXXXXXXXXXXXXXXXXXXXXXXXXXX
9999999    XXXXXXXXXXX    XXXXXXXXXXXXXXXXXXXXXXXXXXXXXXXX
9999999    XXXXXXXXXXX    XXXXXXXXXXXXXXXXXXXXXXXXXXXXXXXX
```

Fig. 11.17

Processing

The program should accept a flight number parameter. This should be used to select all customers who have been booked on to the specified flight.

Details should be output on a report in the format specified.

All errors should be detected and reported.

Initialisation

Open database tables.

If error then
  report the error
  stop run.

Main

Accept the Flight Number parameter.
Retrieve customers specified by the parameter.
While details still to print
  Format a report line.
  If headings required
    print headings.
  Print the report line.
Continue.

Termination

Close the database.
Terminate the program.

Program design

Begin by considering the three main components; data, logical design and the program.

(1) Data. In this case the database! But two tables in particular:

CUSTOMER.
BOOKING.

(2) Logical design. There are two main functions; select the data required and then print it.

(3) The program. COBOL with embedded SQL.

Data

This produces:
CUSTOMER + BOOKING -> Report.

Logical design

See Fig. 11.18.

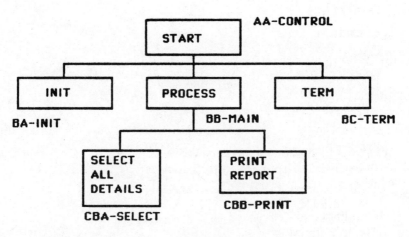

Fig. 11.18

The program

The program itself is actually quite straightforward. If we again follow the recommended approach we build up the code in a series of stages.

The only difficult part of the coding is knowing how to interface the database SQL with the COBOL. Using a previous example, as many programmers do, greatly aids the process.

First consider how SQL can be used. SQL is a query language in its own right. Programmers can type in SQL statements at the prompt which are immediately interpreted and executed on pressing the 'return' key. SQL is very good at extracting information but not so good at manipulating it. This is why simple reports can be written totally in SQL but more complex applications are often written in a third generation language (3GL) such as COBOL to manipulate the data extract, using embedded 4GL statements e.g., SQL.

When you examine the code below, you will see that there is actually very little SQL. Many programmers develop the SQL statements separately and then write the COBOL code around them. Remember that SQL statements can be entered directly into a SQL preprocessor and are executed immediately. This makes it very easy to develop the SQL in isolation before surrounding it by COBOL to enhance it.

Statements beginning with '$$ EXEC' are a way of telling the compiler that what follows is Database/SQL related and not COBOL. The COBOL compiler would ignore these statements and they would be 'compiled' as a separate part of the compilation process. Again note that this implementation will differ from other machines or systems in the way the actual SQL is embedded, see Fig. 11.19.

```
       IDENTIFICATION DIVISION.
       PROGRAM-ID.  FL01.
       AUTHOR.       P.CASIMIR.
       DATE-COMPILED.

      ********************************************************
      *          FLIGHT/CUSTOMERS  REPORT  PROGRAM          *
      *                                                     *
      *    THIS PROGRAM ACTS AS AN EXAMPLE, DESCRIBING      *
      *    THE WAY IN WHICH EMBEDDED SQL STATEMENTS COULD   *
      *    BE USED.                        4/89             *
      ********************************************************
      *   MODS:                                             *
      *   REASON:                                           *
      *   DATE:               VERSION NO:                   *
      ********************************************************
```

continued

Fig. 11.19

```
      ENVIRONMENT DIVISION.
      CONFIGURATION SECTION.
      SOURCE-COMPUTER.   VAX.
      OBJECT-COMPUTER.   VAX.
    *
      INPUT-OUTPUT SECTION.
      FILE-CONTROL.
          SELECT PRINT-FLE ASSIGN LP.
    *
      DATA DIVISION.


      FILE SECTION.
    *
    *
      FD   PRINT-FLE.
          01 PRINT-REC                    PIC X(132).
    *
    *
      WORKING-STORAGE SECTION.
    *
    * DECLARE TABLE COLUMNS.
    *

      01   CUSTOMER.
           03   CUST_NO                    PIC 9(07).
           03   NAME                       PIC X(11).
           03   ADDRESS                    PIC X(30).

      01   BOOKING.
           03   FLIGHT_NO                  PIC X(06).
           03   CUST_NO                    PIC 9(07).
           03   HOTEL                      PIC X(15).
    *
    * DECLARE OTHER VARIABLES.
    *
      01 WS-PAGE                           PIC 9(03) VALUE 1.

      01 WS-DATE.
         03 WS-DD                          PIC 99.
         03 WS-MM                          PIC 99.
         03 WS-YY                          PIC 99.

      01 WS-FLIGHT                         PIC X(06) VALUE
         SPACES.
    *

      01 WS-ERROR-MESSAGE.
         03   WS-PARA                      PIC X(10).
         03   WS-MESSAGE                   PIC X(40).
    *
```

Fig. 11.19 *continued*

```
* PRINT LINES.
*


  01 WS-PRINT-LINE1.
     03  FILLER                              PIC X(50) VALUE
                                                       SPACES.
  01 WS-HEADING-1.
     03  FILLER                              PIC X(07) VALUE
         "SYSTEM ".
     03  FILLER                              PIC X(08) VALUE
         "FLIGHTS ".
     03  FILLER                              PIC X(70) VALUE
         SPACES.
     03  FILLER                              PIC X(05) VALUE
         "PAGE ".
     03  WS-H1-PAGE                          PIC ZZ9.

  01 WS-HEADING-2.
     03  FILLER                              PIC X(05) VALUE
         "DATE ".
     03  WS-H2-DD                            PIC 99    VALUE
         ZEROES.
     03  FILLER                              PIC X(01) VALUE
         "-".
     03  WS-H2-MM                            PIC 99    VALUE
         ZEROES.
     03  FILLER                              PIC X(01) VALUE
         "-".
     03  WS-H2-YY                            PIC 99    VALUE
         ZEROES.
     03  FILLER                              PIC X(60) VALUE
         "           FLIGHTS/CUSTOMERS REPORT "

  01 WS-HEADING-3.
     03  FILLER                              PIC X(60) VALUE
         "                    FOR FLIGHT ".
     03  WS-H3-FLIGHT                        PIC X(06).

  01 WS-HEADING-4.
     03  FILLER                              PIC X(40) VALUE
         SPACES.
     03  FILLER                              PIC X(25) VALUE
         "  -------------------".

  01 WS-HEADING-5.
     03  FILLER                              PIC X(10) VALUE
         "CUST NO. ".
     03  FILLER                              PIC X(10) VALUE
         "  NAME   ".
     03  FILLER                              PIC X(15) VALUE
         "ADDRESS   ".
```

Fig. 11.19 *continued*

```
01 WS-DETAIL.
   03  WS-D-CUST-NO          PIC X(07) VALUE
       SPACES.
   03  FILLER                PIC X(05) VALUE
       SPACES.
   03  WS-D-NAME             PIC X(11) VALUE
       SPACES.
   03  FILLER                PIC X(03) VALUE
       SPACES.
   03  WS-D-ADDRESS          PIC X(30) VALUE
       SPACES.

*
*

   PROCEDURE DIVISION.
   AA-CONTROL SECTION.
   A00-ENTRY.
       PERFORM BA-INIT.
       PERFORM BB-MAIN.
       PERFORM BC-TERM.
       STOP RUN.
   AA99-EXIT.
       EXIT.


   BA-INIT SECTION.
   BA00-ENTRY.

       OPEN OUTPUT PRINT-FLE.

* SET UP DATABASE/COBOL INTERFACE.
* START UP THE STANDARD DATABASE CONTROL PROGRAMS.
* NOTE. $$ INDICATES THE STATEMENT IS SQL, NOT COBOL.

       $$ EXEC DB-HANDLER.
       $$ EXEC ERROR-HANDLER.

* DECLARE THE TABLES TO BE USED.

       $$ EXEC TABLES, BOOKING,CUSTOMER.

* SET UP ERROR HANDLING ROUTINES TO PERFORM IF
* A WARNING STATUS CODE IS RETURNED OR A FATAL
* ERROR OCCURS WHEN EXECUTING A SQL STATEMENT.

       $$ EXEC SQL  ON WARNING PERFORM Z10-WARNING.
       $$ EXEC SQL  ON ERROR   PERFORM Z20-ERROR.

* ACCEPT PARAMETERS.
* AND BACK TO THE COBOL......

       ACCEPT SYS-DATE INTO WS-DATE.
       ACCEPT JCL-PARAM INTO WS-FLIGHT.

       MOVE SPACES TO PRINT-REC.
       MOVE WS-PAGE TO WS-H1-PAGE.
       MOVE WS-DD TO WS-H2-DD.
       MOVE WS-MM TO WS-H2-MM.
       MOVE WS-YY TO WS-H2-YY.
```

Fig. 11.19 *continued*

```
* PRINT REPORT HEADINGS ONCE.

        MOVE WS-FLIGHT TO WS-H3-FLIGHT.

        MOVE WS-HEADING-1 TO PRINT-REC.
        WRITE PRINT-REC AFTER PAGE.
        MOVE WS-HEADING-2 TO PRINT-REC.
        WRITE PRINT-REC AFTER PAGE.
        MOVE WS-HEADING-3 TO PRINT-REC.
        WRITE PRINT-REC AFTER PAGE.
        MOVE WS-HEADING-4 TO PRINT-REC.
        WRITE PRINT-REC AFTER PAGE.
        MOVE WS-HEADING-5 TO PRINT-REC.
        WRITE PRINT-REC AFTER PAGE.

    BA99-EXIT.
        EXIT.




    BB-MAIN SECTION.
    BB00-ENTRY.

        MOVE "BB00-ENTRY " TO WS-PARA.
        MOVE "SQL ERROR"    TO WS-MESSAGE.


        PERFORM CBA-SELECT.

        PERFORM CBB-PRINT UNTIL EOT.

    BB99-EXIT.
        EXIT.




    BC-TERM SECTION.
    BC00-ENTRY.
        MOVE "BB00-ENTRY " TO WS-PARA.
        MOVE "SQL ERROR"    TO WS-MESSAGE.

        CLOSE PRINT-FLE.

        $$ EXEC CLOSE.
    BC99-EXIT.
        EXIT.


    CBA-SELECT SECTION.
    CBA00-ENTRY.

* SELECT ALL CUSTOMERS FOR SPECIFIED FLIGHT.

        MOVE "CBA00-ENTRY"   TO WS-PARA.
        MOVE "SELECT ERROR " TO WS-MESSAGE.

        $$ EXEC SQL BEGIN.
```

Fig. 11.19 *continued*

```
        SELECT CUSTOMER.CUST_NO,NAME,ADDRESS
            FROM CUSTOMER, BOOKING
        WHERE BOOKING.CUST_NO = CUSTOMER.CUST_NO

            AND BOOKING.FLIGHT_NO = WS-FLIGHT

    $$ EXEC SQL END.

 * IF NOT FOUND THEN CONTROL HAS JUMPED TO Z10-WARNING

    CBA99-EXIT.
        EXIT.



    CBB-PRINT SECTION.
    CBB00-ENTRY.

 * PRINT ALL CUSTOMER DETAILS.

        MOVE "CBB00-ENTRY"   TO WS-PARA.
        MOVE "USAGE ERROR "  TO WS-MESSAGE.

        MOVE CUST_NO   TO WS-D-CUST-NO.
        MOVE NAME TO        WS-D-NAME.
        MOVE ADDRESS TO     WS-D-ADDRESS.

        MOVE WS-DETAIL TO PRINT-REC.
        WRITE PRINT-REC AFTER 1.

    CBB99-EXIT.
        EXIT.



    Z10-WARNING SECTION.
    Z10-ENTRY.
 *      NO RECORDS FOUND, DISPLAY MESSAGE AND END.

        DISPLAY "WARNING - RECS. NOT FOUND.     ".
        $$ EXEC CLOSE
        STOP RUN.
    Z10-EXIT.
        EXIT.


    Z20-ERROR SECTION.
    Z20-ENTRY.
 *      A FATAL SQL ERROR HAS OCCURRED, DISPLAY MESSAGE
 *      AND END.

        DISPLAY WS-ERROR-MESSAGE.
        $$ EXEC CLOSE
        STOP RUN.
    Z20-EXIT.
        EXIT.
```

Fig. 11.19 *continued*

Note When compiling programs with embedded SQL, there are generally three stages. The first identifies all the SQL and database statements and pre-processes them. The second stage compiles the program while the third stage links all the separate executable components together.

Program testing

Although embedded database statements (SQL) are combined with standard COBOL statements, the program is still a standard batch job. It should therefore be tested in much the same way as any other program.

Think how you would test this program. How would you check the SQL statement was correct? Would timing a program run be part of your testing, to measure performance? Would it be useful to 'prove' the SQL on its own as well as within the program? Try deciding on other questions to ask yourself if you were to be passed the above program to test, see Figs 11.20 and 11.21.

(a) Identifying paths and conditions.
(b) Creating test data.
(c) Producing a test script.
(d) Testing, amending and documenting.

It can be useful to detail the actual input test data, in this case the table

TEST SCRIPT.   SYSTEM: FLIGHT   PROGRAM: FLO1

TEST ID DATE	INPUT	CONDITION	EXPECTED	ACTUAL

Fig. 11.20

TEST SCRIPT.   SYSTEM: FLIGHT   PROGRAM: FLO1

TEST ID DATE	INPUT	CONDITION	EXPECTED	ACTUAL
Database opened.	–	–	Database accessed.	
Data Param accepted.	System date.	–	Date accepted.	
Flight No accepted.	Flight No.	–	Flight No received.	
Correct customer data selected.	Database	Selection correct.	Correct data.	

Fig. 11.21

contents, and also the expected output information.

Database systems, and specifically relational database organisations using SQL are becoming increasingly widely used. Such systems give greater data flexibility and are attracting the introduction of highly sophisticated development tools. COBOL still has a part to play in the use of this new technology. A knowledge of SQL and COBOL is however, a great strength.

CHAPTER 12

The development of a screen based SQL system

This next example looks at a different type of application; a screen based system using SQL.

In creating programs for this larger system, the day-to-day realities of working in a team and personal time management will also be addressed.

Again, five different stages are addressed; the program specification, program design, structured programming, writing to standards and testing. So that we can begin, you will need an overview of the system.

System overview

Equipment maintenance companies now exist to take on the maintenance of personal computers, for commercial organisations. Annual premiums are paid and in return such companies provide engineer support on-site and

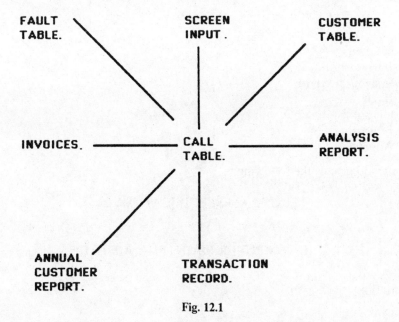

FAULT TABLE.

SCREEN INPUT.

CUSTOMER TABLE.

INVOICES.

CALL TABLE.

ANALYSIS REPORT.

ANNUAL CUSTOMER REPORT.

TRANSACTION RECORD.

Fig. 12.1

within a specified time limit. This system is used to record such telephoned faults, recording required details for use in scheduling engineers' time and marketing analysis of faults recorded, see Fig. 12.1.

Program specification

Using our standard program specification we can write a specification for the first of the required programs.

The first program is required to allow the insertion, deletion, amendment and querying of faults, held on the faults table. In addition to this first program, a second program is also required to print a hard-copy (paper) of the screen based transaction. This second program, acting as an audit-trail record, is to be 'called' automatically by the first. Two different people are to work on each program.

Other programs are also required to produce invoices and analysis reports. Because of the urgency of the system, a number of programmers will be working as a team on the project.

Working in a team on a time constrained project demands effective time management on a personal and project basis. It also requires effective communication amongst team members, both in terms of work being done and work completed, more of this later.

For our first program, the screen program, we can start with the basic program specification outline.

Program specification skeleton

(1) Contents
(2) Introduction
(3) System flowchart
(4) Input
(5) Output
(6) Processing
(7) Appendix

This could give us the following:

PROGRAM SPECIFICATION.

SCR01.

ACME COMPUTER MAINTENANCE LTD.

Contents

(1) Contents

(2) Introduction
(3) System flowchart
(4) Input
(5) Output
(6) Processing
(7) Appendix

Introduction

SCR01 forms part of the customer fault reporting system. Customers can query the status of faults already reported or report new fault details. They can also request that fault details be corrected or removed.

Details recorded are shown on the screen layout. To save file space, the customer name and address are referenced from a separate customer table, accessed by customer number. If the customer is a new one then a record is automatically created on the customer table.

Entity diagram

See Fig. 12.2.

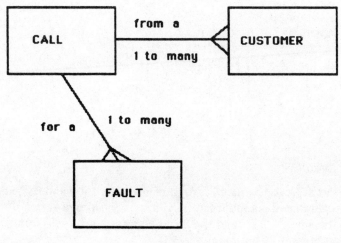

Fig. 12.2

Tables

The following files are used:

CUSTOMER TABLE.
CALL TABLE.
FAULT TABLE.

Also required is the screen layout as shown in Fig. 12.3.

CUSTOMER TABLE.

CUST_NO	NAME	ADDRESS	BALANCE

FAULT TABLE

FAULT_NO	DESC.	SCHEDULE Y/N	BY	DELETE

CALL TABLE

CUST_NO	FAULT_NO

Fig. 12.3

Screen layout

As an exercise, read Chapter 4 (Program characteristics) and try to design a usable and well laid out input screen. Consider the idea of screen simplicity, the way the screen will be used and the order information will be entered. Try to cut screen input to a minimum.

Begin by deciding the screen headings. Perhaps use each top and bottom half of the screen to represent customer and fault details respectively. Use Xs to represent data fields.

Processing

The function of this program is to allow the recording and maintenance of telephone-reported faults. Fault details can be entered, amended and deleted via an input screen.

Details are later scheduled for repair by an engineer scheduling program. Once a screen based transaction is completed, it should be printed by a separately called module.

Initialisation

Open tables.
If there an Open error
   display an error message,
   stop run.
Capture the Screen Operator's initials into
   BY.
Clear all screen fields.

Main

On Insertion of a record:

Create a new fault number
   i.e. Increment the greatest number by 1.
Request and attempt to match the
   customer number/details.
If a new customer then
   create a new customer number
   and add customer record and details.
Create the fault record
   and display the fault number.
Create the Call record.

On Amendment:

Retrieve the record using the fault number.
Allow amendment on all but the key field.
Update the record.
Note that the original BY field should not
   allow amendments to be made.

On Deletion:

Set the DELETED field to 'Y' on the fault record
   but do not physically delete the record.
Rewrite the record.
Delete the Call record for the FAULT_NO.
Print the screen.

Termination

Close all tables and clear the screen.
Terminate the program.

So far, a series of well defined steps have been taken to arrive at the current point. At each stage it has been possible to create a deliverable i.e., a physical result of your actions. The implications of this approach are that at every stage you know exactly what you have done and produced and what is still outstanding.

If working in a team on a project, the project should have been planned in terms of deliverables and timescales by your project manager. This involves being able to say that, 'in 25 days' time, three of the five programs should be at the testing stage'.

If your manager asks how you are doing, telling him your program is 'nearly finished' is like saying the channel tunnel is nearly finished – it says nothing! Conversely, if you were to say that you 'had only the testing and documentation to tidy, which should take two days' then you are providing real management information! In addition, if you can manage your own time then you are well on the way to managing other people's as well!

How to manage your time? One proven method is the use of simple Gantt charts to plan and record predicted against actual events and time. Sounds confusing? The method is really very simple, see Fig. 12.4.

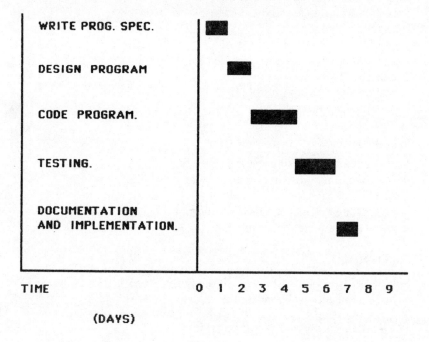

Fig. 12.4

Time required for each defined event is shown. Work from top-to-bottom, left-to-right. Mark events as they are completed to show clearly the progress of what you are working on.

A useful technique which should really only be used as a guideline is the idea of estimating the time required to write a program. Just one of the many approaches to this idea follows.

Program time estimation

Scheduling any task is not an easy exercise. If you are applying the principles of time management then you will already have discovered how difficult it can sometimes be to estimate time. Accurate program estimation has an important part to play however, in the overall scheduling process.

Some people believe in program estimation and others do not. By program estimation we mean the time taken to complete a program from the point of handing over the program specification to having it ready for implementation.

Many formulae exist to help achieve realistic figures. Additionally some people work on the basis of a four day week to allow for other unforeseen considerations. Others again think of a figure and then double it! This might appear a little extreme but think how many projects you know of that have come in on time. Of course, some logic has to be applied to the exercise, especially if the estimates are for an outside client or interested senior managers. One does not want to make the estimates too generous and appear inefficient nor make them too tight and risk disappointment later.

Many factors affect the process; speed of hardware, development environment, staff experience, learning curves, business knowledge and so on.

Most actual estimation formulae rate the experience of the programmer, the program complexity, program type and program size.

For example a method might add the three considerations above and multiply by the programmer experience factor.

The end result should be an estimate in days.

$$((C + T + S) * E) * 1.2 = DAYS$$

where C is the complexity, T the type, S the program size and
E the programmer experience.

These three considerations could all be rated from 1 to 5, and experience 2.0 to 0.5 for the more experienced programmer.

This is by no means a definitive method but simply illustrates the type of method often used. The results could simply be used as a guideline and used in conjunction with general programming/estimating experience. Be careful, however, many people measure their own performance purely on the way they reach estimates or not. Take this into consideration when assigning them. It is better to deliver late and working than on time but inadequately tested.

This idea is simple but powerful. Remember that it is not only when writing programs that you can plan with Gantt charts and program estimates. They also could be used when developing a project, building a house or planning a wedding!

Program design

Begin by considering the three main components; data, logical design and the program.

(1) Data
   Customer Table – In/Out.
   Fault Table   – In/Out.
   Call Table   – In/Out.
   Screen print   – Out.

CUSTOMER TABLE

CUST_NO	NAME	ADDRESS	BALANCE
452	BA PLC	4, THE ROAD	4567
341	ACME	3, OLD LANE	560

FAULT TABLE

FAULT_NO	DESC.	SCHEDULE Y/N	BY	DELETE
77	MONITOR	Y	PL	N
79	DISK	N	CV	N
89	MODEM	Y	PL	N

CALL TABLE

CUST_NO	FAULT_NO
452	77
452	89
341	79

Fig. 12.5

(2) Logical design
Random processing of rows.
(3) The program
Use a box and line diagram.
Map boxes onto Sections.
Detail the Identification and Environment Divisions.
Write the Data Division and outline the Working-Storage.
Complete the main areas of code.

Data

See Fig. 12.5.

Logical design

This is more complicated as, so far, we have only arrived at Fig. 12.6. However, with our design specification we have already defined the three major functions, i.e., insertion, amendment and deletion.

Further refining the diagram at a function level is easy.

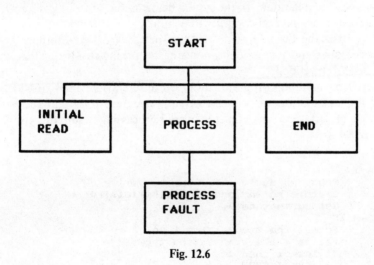

Fig. 12.6

The program

Using the three functions defined we arrive at Fig. 12.7. Note that the lack of any serial processing allows processing to be defined in a more isolated way. Individual functions tend not be related and there is less of a feeling of flow of data. Note section names have been added.

The three functions are quite distinct. The only other major issue is how

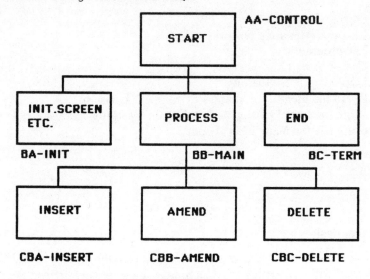

Fig. 12.7

the actual screen handling of the system being used works. This differs from machine to machine and compiler to compiler.

Now write the Data Division and outline the Working-Storage. Again, some compilers use a screen definition area in working-storage, so this would also need to be coded.

As screen handling programs differ on different machines so widely in their implementation we will not actually code the program. Instead an example of code, used to define the overall processing required is given, see Fig. 12.8.

```
BA-INIT
        Open tables.
        Capture screen operators initials.
        Get current date.
BB-MAIN
        Accept the transaction type.
        Validate the transaction type.
        If Insert then do
            CBA-INSERT
        Enddo
        If Amendment then do
            CBB-AMEND
        Enddo
        If Deletion then do
            CBC-DELETE
        Enddo
            else
        Error.
```

Fig. 12.8

BC-TERM
> Close tables.
> Clear screen fields.
> Stop.

CBA-INSERT.
> Clear screen.
> If no customer supplied customer number then do
>> Accept Customer Name/Address
>> Allocate new Customer number
>> Set balance to zero
>> Write Customer record.
>
> Else
>> Accept Customer Number
>> Read Customer record
>> Display Customer details.
>
> Enddo
> Accept Fault details.
> Generate new Fault number.
> Create Fault record.
> Display Fault recorded confirmation message.
> Create Call record.
> Print Screen.

CBB-AMEND
> Accept Fault number.
> Retrieve required record.
> If found then do
>> Clear screen
>> Display record
>> Allow update of non-protected fields on
>>> screen
>> Rewrite record
>> Print Screen.
>
> Else
>> Display record not found message.
>
> Enddo

CBC-DELETE
> Accept Fault number.
> Retrieve required record.
> If found then do
>> Clear screen
>> Display record
>> Set deleted indicator to 'Y'
>> Rewrite record
>> Delete Call record.
>> Print Screen.
>
> Else
>> Display record not found message.
>
> Enddo

Fig. 12.8 *continued*

As an exercise you should try to write the SQL parts of the above program against the above outline.

Use the existing examples of SQL as a guide. Most useful will be your attempts to code the SQL that extracts data from the tables, for example, searching for an existing record or inserting a new one.

Program testing

How do you go about testing a screen based program?

The overall approach should still include the four basic considerations i.e.,

(a) Identifying paths and conditions.
(b) Creating test data.
(c) Producing a test script.
(d) Testing, amending and documenting.

Actual testing is quite similar to a batch based program. What is not so easy is the recording of the test results when proving such things as screen handling. Some systems allow the connection of screen printers, printers that will print exactly what is shown on the screen. If this is not the case then testing is still possible but documentation of results will take longer.

Use the test script below to define questions you might ask when testing the above program. Examples could include attempting to update the fault number (not allowed) or checking that fault records created were pointing to the correct customer record.

Produce the test script

This can be done using a standard test script form, see Fig. 12.9.

TEST SCRIPT. SYSTEM: MAILING PROGRAM: SCRO1				
TEST ID	INPUT	CONDITION	EXPECTED	ACTUAL

Fig. 12.9

The program has been designed, coded and written, testing completed and the program is ready to become part of the overall fault recording system.

What if other more junior members of your team had not written a screen based program before? Would the use of a structured walkthrough be a useful way of explaining the techniques to them? Probably yes. So how would you go about organising such a meeting? Check the chapter on structured walkthroughs and plan an approach to such a meeting.

In this case the subject would be you and your program. The chairman could be your team leader along with two or three of your peers. Prior to the meeting you could circulate copies of your program source. It could also be useful to set up a screen in the meeting room to talk through the screen-based programming functions you had used.

So to complete the writing of this program by presenting its working to your colleagues you could:

(1) Arrange a walkthrough.
(2) Set a time and venue.
(3) Circulate the source code plus screen layouts.
(4) Appoint a chairman.
(5) Arrange the use of a computer terminal.

By holding such a meeting you would be informing others of what you had learnt and providing an alternative to expensive formal training. This is an example of when a walkthrough is truly useful as a forum for learning.

A SQL report

This next example looks at a different type of application; a SQL report using only SQL and relational database tables.

Three different stages are addressed; the program specification, program design and testing. So that we can begin, we will need an overview of the system.

System overview

The table description in Fig. 13.1 describes house details as they could be recorded by an estate agent.

HOUSES TABLE

HOUSE NO	ADDRESS	TYPE	COST	STATUS

Fig. 13.1

HOUSES TABLE

HOUSE NO	ADDRESS	TYPE	COST	STATUS
56	OLD LANE	SEMI	89,000	OPEN
23A	ACORNS	BUNG	75,000	OFFER
102	RIPON WAY	DET	99,950	OPEN
45	MILFORD CL	1 BED	75,500	EXCH
FLAT B	GREEN LANE	2 BED	82,750	OPEN

Fig. 13.2

Each row represents the details of one house. The table is used by the estate agent to record such details and can be updated or queried using only SQL.

It could be populated as shown in Fig. 13.2.

Program specification

SQL is performed or executed differently from COBOL. Each statement is executed in turn. There is no direct concept of a GO TO statement and general formatting of data can be difficult. Conversely, it can be very easy to extract information quickly without having to write reams of code.

Remember, the basic syntax of a SQL statement is SELECT data FROM tables WHERE a condition is true.

Program specification skeleton

(1) Contents
(2) Introduction
(3) System flowchart
(4) Input
(5) Output
(6) Processing
(7) Appendix

This could give us the following:

PROGRAM SPECIFICATION.

HSE01.

GAZUMP AND RUN ESTATE AGENTS LTD.

Contents

(1) Contents
(2) Introduction
(3) System flowchart
(4) Input
(5) Output
(6) Processing
(7) Appendix

Introduction

HSE01 forms part of the general estate agents' housing list enquiry and update system.

Data are held on all houses whether for sale or in the process of being sold. Their main purpose is to supply details of houses to potential clients. House details can be extracted on a number of different house attributes.

System flowchart

HSE01

HOUSES TABLE

Input–Output

The table shown in Fig. 13.3. is used:

HOUSES TABLE

HOUSE NO	ADDRESS	TYPE	COST	STATUS

Fig. 13.3

Processing

The purpose of the program is to select data from the HOUSES table that matches the supplied parameters, or any combination of them.

Type, cost and status can all be matched.

Initialisation

In SQL there is no real concept of initialisation. This will become apparent by studying the SQL shown and recognising that parameters are only obtained when actually referred to in the SQL. At that moment they will be automatically prompted for by the system.

Main

Select all House No, Address, Type, Cost, Status
which match Type and are less than the
specified cost and are of status OPEN.
Display all details.

Termination

Close the table.

Program design

Program design in SQL can become an almost non-existent process. Again, by remembering the basic syntax of SELECT data FROM table WHERE condition, the program is nearly complete.

However, if you have ever come across any SQL statements you will soon realise how complex and difficult to understand they can become. This is often because complex SQL begins as a simple statement and is then added to, introducing additional nesting of SELECTS and sub-queries. The SELECT statement becomes larger and larger and more difficult to maintain.

Referring back to an earlier sub-query, we used the example of:

```
SELECT EMPLOYEE_NO, EMPLOYEE_NAME
    FROM EMPLOYEE
    WHERE JOB_TYPE =
        ( SELECT JOB_TYPE
          FROM CAREER
          WHERE SALARY_LIMIT > 15000 )
```

We might have developed this SQL by first creating it as:

```
SELECT EMPLOYEE_NO, EMPLOYEE_NAME
    FROM EMPLOYEE
    WHERE JOB_TYPE =
        ( SELECT A )
```

We could then develop the SQL to SELECT the required job types to be substituted for 'A'.

By using this semi top-down approach, not only do we ease the task of developing more complex SQL but we also show the growth of the statement which could act as very useful documentation. If the SQL statement was found to be at fault, breaking down the SQL into its individual SELECT components would make testing and debugging much more simple.

The design of SQL is still not a well defined process. This is partly due to the fact that SQL is a query language. It is not designed as a language with which to develop large complex programs. If the application becomes complicated then another language should also be used, COBOL with embedded SQL statements being an ideal choice.

We return to our SQL program. It is a very simple program to write. The specification gives us all the detail we really need. Writing the SQL is a formality.

Select all House No, Address, Type, Cost, Status
which match Type and is less or equal to the
specified cost are of status OPEN.

HOUSES TABLE

HOUSE NO	ADDRESS	TYPE	COST	STATUS

```
SELECT HOUSE_NO, ADDRESS, TYPE, COST, STATUS
    FROM HOUSE
    WHERE ( &TYPE = TYPE ) AND
          ( COST BETWEEN 0 AND &COST ) AND
          ( STATUS = 'OPEN' )
```

Note that & denotes a user enterable variable.

This program is very simple, but imagine the length of the program and the time to write it if it was written in COBOL using conventional file structures.

Running it on the houses table would produce the result shown in Fig. 13.4.

Running the SQL job, see Fig. 13.5.

HOUSES TABLE

HOUSE NO	ADDRESS	TYPE	COST	STATUS
56	OLD LANE	SEMI	89,000	OPEN
23A	ACORNS	BUNG	75,000	OFFER
102	RIPON WAY	DET	99,950	OPEN
45	MILFORD CL	1 BED	75,500	EXCH
FLAT B	GREEN LANE	2 BED	82,750	OPEN

Fig. 13.4

TYPE?	You enter	SEMI	
COST?	You enter	90,000	

gives

HOUSE_NO	ADDRESS	TYPE	COST	STATUS
FLAT B	GREEN LANE	SEMI	82,750	OPEN
56	OLD LANE	SEMI	89,000	OPEN

Fig. 13.5

Program testing

How do you go about testing a SQL program?

The overall approach should still include the four basic considerations i.e.,

(a) Identifying paths and conditions.
(b) Creating test data.
(c) Producing a test script.
(d) Testing, amending and documenting.

Testing SQL is not always easy but by following the four standard steps it can be better organised.

Identifying paths and conditions is very important. If a top-down approach has be taken regarding more complex SQL then each section of SQL can be tested individually as well as in its entirety.

The creation of test data should be done in exactly the same way as for any other language. Attempt to create a true mix of data. SQL select statements can be made up of many AND and OR conditions. Enough test data should be created to cater for each of these conditions.

The creation of a test script, in the standard format, and testing follows the standard testing path.

Writing SQL programs can at times appear quite an unstructured process. The nature of the language dictates this. Remember however that SQL can still be developed, documented and tested in a controlled manner. Stand-alone SQL programs are still not very common. COBOL with embedded SQL statements are much more widely used and can therefore be developed using the traditional design, coding and testing guidelines.

CHAPTER 14

A COBOL/SQL car insurance and quotation system

System overview

This system is used to record details of car insurance quotations and any subsequently recorded insurance policies.

Details are updated and viewed both interactively via a screen and by batch report production. Three levels of detail are recorded. These are the customer details such as name and address, the quotation details including the car type and cost and then any actual policy taken up, including expiry date etc.

The data is held on a relational database and is accessed using SQL and embedded SQL statements with COBOL.

Program specification

PROGRAM SPECIFICATION.

INS01.

MULTIPLE QUOTATIONS LTD.

Contents

(1) Contents
(2) Introduction
(3) System flowchart
(4) Input
(5) Output
(6) Processing
(7) Appendix

Introduction

INS01 forms part of the Quotation and Policy Car Insurance System. Its function is to convert existing insurance quotations into fully paid insurance policies. The program is to be run in batch mode and is an update program.

The program is to be run as an overnight database update job. It uses three database tables; CUSTOMER, QUOTATION and POLICY.

Entity–relationship diagram

See Fig. 14.1

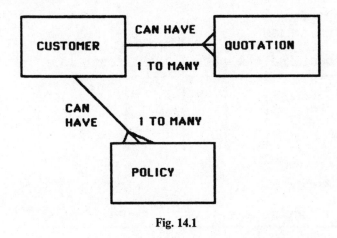

Fig. 14.1

Input–output

See Fig. 14.2

QUOTATIONS/POLICIES Database.

Tables: CUSTOMER, QUOTATION, POLICY.

Processing

The function of the program is to convert all 'taken-up' car insurance quotations and create new policy entries.

Scan all entries in the quotations table and update each entry with the YES indicator set to 'Y'. Create a new policy entry and update the Customer LIVE indicator to 'Y'.

After each new policy creation, commit the new entry as a discrete piece of work. In the event of an update failure rollback the current unit of work and continue processing.

Report any processing errors.

Initialisation

Open database tables.

CUSTOMER

CUST_NO	NAME	ADDRESS	LIVE

QUOTATION

QUOTE_NO	CAR	NCB	COST	CUST_NO	YES

POLICY

POLICY_NO	CAR	COST	EXPIRY	CUST_NO

Fig. 14.2

Lock the POLICY table.
If error then
   report the error
   stop run.
Obtain todays date.

Main

Select the next Quotations entry.
If the YES indicator = Y then
   Select the associated Customer
   Set the Customer to LIVE = Y.
   Select the next Policy Number
      i.e. increment the greatest by 1.

Update the Policy table with a new entry.
Update the Quotations indicator by setting it to = OK.
Continue.

Termination

Close the database.
Terminate the program.

Program design

See Fig. 14.3.

Note It is perhaps worth mentioning a number of features included in the following program. Not only does the program both select information from the database as well as update it, it performs two other functions as well.

Firstly, the program 'locks' the policies table. Locking is a feature of some database systems. It allows the programmer to restrict access to all or part of a database so that particular operations, usually updates, can be performed with full data integrity. In relational databases sometimes just a specified row will be locked, on other occasions the entire table will be locked. Some locks allow read only access on data for other users. Other locks can limit any access to all other users.

Why lock? There are occasions when data needs to be accessed, lengthy calculations performed and the data then perhaps rewritten. If, in-between reading the data and rewriting it, another user were perhaps to also read and update the data, the results could be very serious – major inconsistencies in the data.

The second feature of the program is the way it commits data. Committing data means writing the data totally to the database. Before data is

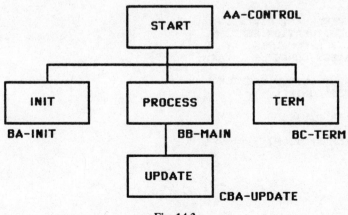

Fig. 14.3

committed, the potential changes about to be made can be reversed or 'rolled back'. Some database systems use the idea of a logical unit of work i.e., continually committing small amounts of data. In the event of a program failure only the most current unit of work would be lost i.e., not committed, see Fig. 14.4.

```
       IDENTIFICATION DIVISION.
       PROGRAM-ID. INS01.
       AUTHOR.     P.CASIMIR.
       DATE-COMPILED.

       ******************************************************
       *          FLIGHT/CUSTOMERS REPORT PROGRAM           *
       *                                                    *
       *    THIS PROGRAM UPDATES THE CUSTOMER, QUOTATIONS   *
       *    AND POLICIES TABLE BY CONVERTING QUOTATIONS     *
       *    TO LIVE POLICIES.                               *
       ******************************************************
       *    MODS:                                           *
       *    REASON:                                         *
       *    DATE:             VERSION NO:                   *
       ******************************************************

       * PROGRAM STRUCTURE:
       *
       *    AA-CONTROL
       *         I
       *         I
       *         I-BA-INIT
       *         I
       *         I-BB-MAIN
       *         I       I
       *         I       I
       *         I           ---CBA-UPDATE
       *         I
       *         I-BC-TERM
       *
       ******************************************************
       *

       ENVIRONMENT DIVISION.
       CONFIGURATION SECTION.
       SOURCE-COMPUTER.    VAX.
       OBJECT-COMPUTER.    VAX.
       *
       INPUT-OUTPUT SECTION.
       FILE-CONTROL.
      .*
       DATA DIVISION.
       *
       FILE SECTION.
       *
       *
```

Fig. 14.4

```
WORKING-STORAGE SECTION.
*
* DECLARE TABLE COLUMNS.
*


01   CUSTOMER.
     03   C_CUST_NO                PIC 9(09).
     03   C_NAME                   PIC X(25).
     03   C_ADDRESS_1              PIC X(25).
     03   C_ADDRESS_2              PIC X(25).
     03   C_ADDRESS_3              PIC X(25).
     03   C_LIVE                   PIC X(01).


01   QUOTATION.
     03   Q_QUOTE_NO               PIC 9(09).
     03   Q_CAR                    PIC X(12).
     03   Q_NCB                    PIC 9(01).
     03   Q_COST                   PIC 9999V99.
     03   Q_CUST_NO                PIC 9(09).
     03   Q_YES                    PIC X(02).


01   POLICY.
     03   P_POLICY_NO              PIC 9(09).
     03   P_CAR                    PIC X(12).
     03   P_COST                   PIC 9999V99.
     03   P_EXPIRY_DATE            PIC 9(06).
     03   P_CUST_NO                PIC 9(09).


*
* DECLARE OTHER VARIABLES.
*

* TEMPORARY TABLE STORAGE.


01   WS-QUOTATION.
     03   WS_QUOTE_NO              PIC 9(09).
     03   WS_CAR                   PIC X(12).
     03   WS_NCB                   PIC 9(01).
     03   WS_COST                  PIC 9999V99.
     03   WS_CUST_NO               PIC 9(09).
     03   WS_YES                   PIC X(02).

01   WS-NEXT-POLICY-NO            PIC 9(09) VALUE
                                            ZEROES.

01 WS-DATE.
   03 WS-DD                       PIC 99.
   03 WS-MM                       PIC 99.
   03 WS-YY                       PIC 99.

*


01 WS-ERROR-MESSAGE.
   03   WS-PARA                   PIC X(10).
   03   WS-MESSAGE                PIC X(40).
*
*
*
```

Fig. 14.4 *continued*

```
       PROCEDURE DIVISION.
       AA-CONTROL SECTION.
       A00-ENTRY.
           PERFORM BA-INIT.
           PERFORM BB-MAIN.
           PERFORM BC-TERM.
           STOP RUN.
       AA99-EXIT.
           EXIT.


       BA-INIT SECTION.
       BA00-ENTRY.

       DISPLAY "VERSION  1.00 ".

 *  SET UP DATABASE/COBOL INTERFACE.
 *  START UP THE STANDARD DATABASE CONTROL PROGRAMS.

           $$ EXEC DB-HANDLER.
           $$ EXEC ERROR-HANDLER.

 *  DECLARE THE TABLES TO BE USED.

           $$ EXEC TABLES,CUSTOMER,QUOTATION,POLICY.

 *  SET UP ERROR HANDLING ROUTINES TO PERFORM IF
 *  A WARNING STATUS CODE IS RETURNED OR A FATAL
 *  ERROR OCCURS WHEN EXECUTING A SQL STATEMENT.

           $$ EXEC SQL  ON WARNING PERFORM Z10-WARNING.
           $$ EXEC SQL  ON ERROR    PERFORM Z20-ERROR.

 *  LOCK THE POLICIES TABLE.

           $   EXEC LOCK TABLE POLICY.
           $   EXEC SQL  ON ERROR   PERFORM Z20-ERROR.

 *  ACCEPT TODAYS DATE.

           ACCEPT SYS-DATE INTO WS-DATE.

       BA99-EXIT.
           EXIT.



       BB-MAIN SECTION.
       BB00-ENTRY.

           MOVE "BB00-ENTRY " TO WS-PARA.
           MOVE "SQL ERROR"   TO WS-MESSAGE.


           PERFORM CBA-UPDATE.


       BB99-EXIT.
           EXIT.
```

Fig. 14.4 *continued*

```
BC-TERM SECTION.
BC00-ENTRY.
    MOVE "BB00-ENTRY " TO WS-PARA.
    MOVE "SQL ERROR"   TO WS-MESSAGE.

* CLOSE THE DATABASE TABLES.

    $$ EXEC CLOSE.
BC99-EXIT.
    EXIT.


  CBA-UPDATE SECTION.
  CBA00-ENTRY.

* PROCESS QUOTATIONS.

  CBA10-NEXT-QUOTATION.

* SELECT JUST ONE ROW WHERE THE YES INDICATOR
* IS EQUAL TO Y. I.E. READ NEXT RECORD.

  CBA20-QUOTE.

    MOVE "CBA20-QUOTE"  TO WS-PARA.
    MOVE "SELECT ERROR " TO WS-MESSAGE.

    $$ EXEC SQL BEGIN.

        SELECT *,COUNT(*) INTO
            WS_QUOTE_NO,
            WS_CAR,
            WS_NCB,
            WS_COST,
            WS_CUST_NO,
            WS_YES
        FROM QUOTATION
        WHERE Q_YES = 'Y'
            GROUP BY Q_YES
            HAVING COUNT(*) = 1

    $$ EXEC SQL END.


* SET THE CUSTOMER LIVE INDICATOR TO
* 'Y' AS THE CUSTOMER WILL HAVE A VALID
* POLICY ASSOCIATED WITH HIM.

  CBA30-CUST.

    MOVE "CBA30-CUST "  TO WS-PARA.
    MOVE "SET ERROR    " TO WS-MESSAGE.

    $$ EXEC SQL BEGIN.

        UPDATE CUSTOMER
        SET LIVE = 'Y'
        WHERE CUSTOMER.CUST_NO = QUOTATION.CUST_NO
            AND QUOTATION.QUOTE_NO = WS_QUOTE_NO
```

Fig. 14.4 *continued*

```
            $$ EXEC SQL END

       * GET THE NEXT POLICY NUMBER TO USE

       CBA40-POLICY-NO.

            MOVE "CBA40-POLICY"  TO WS-PARA.
            MOVE "SELECT ERROR " TO WS-MESSAGE.

            $$ EXEC SQL BEGIN
                SELECT MAX( POLICY_NO)
                    INTO WS-NEXT-POLICY-NO
                    FROM POLICY

            $$ EXEC SQL END

            ADD 1 TO WS-NEXT-POLICY-NO.

       * GENERATE POLICY EXPIRY DATE.

            ADD 1 TO WS-YY.

       CBA50-POLICY.

            MOVE "CBA50-POLICY"  TO WS-PARA.
            MOVE "INSERT ERROR " TO WS-MESSAGE.

            $$ SQL BEGIN

                INSERT INTO POLICY
                    VALUES ( WS-NEXT-POLICY-NO,
                             WS_CAR,
                             WS_COST,
                             WS_DATE,
                             WS_CUST_NO )

            $$ SQL END

       * SET QUOTATIONS YES INDICATOR TO YES

       CBA60-QUOTE.

            MOVE "CBA60-QUOTE"   TO WS-PARA.
            MOVE "UPDATE ERROR " TO WS-MESSAGE.

            $$ SQL BEGIN

                UPDATE QUOTATION
                    SET YES = 'OK'
                    WHERE QUOTE_NO = WS_QUOTE_NO

            COMMIT

            $$ SQL END

            GO TO CBA-NEXT-QUOTATION.

       CBA99-EXIT.
          EXIT.
```

Fig. 14.4 *continued*

```
Z10-WARNING SECTION.
Z10-ENTRY.
*       NO RECORDS FOUND, DISPLAY MESSAGE AND END.

        DISPLAY "WARNING - RECS. NOT FOUND.     ".
        $$ EXEC CLOSE
        STOP RUN.
Z10-EXIT.
        EXIT.


Z20-ERROR SECTION.
Z20-ENTRY.
*       A FATAL SQL ERROR HAS OCCURRED, DISPLAY MESSAGE
*       AND ROLLBACK THEN END.

        DISPLAY WS-ERROR-MESSAGE.
        $$ ROLLBACK
        $$ EXEC CLOSE
        STOP RUN.
Z20-EXIT.
        EXIT.
```

Fig. 14.4 *continued*

The program is now complete. The SQL statements, although quite short are at times quite sophisticated and perhaps require a little explanation.

- CBA20-QUOTE. This SQL statement uses an asterisk * to say select everything within the row. COUNT(*) counts the number of rows returned, which could be more than one. However by specifying the HAVING COUNT(*) = 1, then only the first row to meet the selection condition is returned.
- CBA30-CUST. This statement updates a column within a row where the condition is true for two table entries matching together. Note that a working-storage field is used as part of the condition test.
- CBA40-POLICY-NO. MAX returns the maximum figure from all the selected rows accessed i.e., just one figure.
- CBA50-POLICY. A new row is being inserted into the policies table.

The previous example shows a variety of ways in which SQL can be used to access and update relational database tables.

Combining SQL with COBOL becomes a very powerful tool and paves the way for ensuring the future of COBOL as a commercial development language.

Summary

Being a good COBOL programmer requires many skills: understanding a program specification, planning the structure of the program, defining the logic all before the coding even begins, then the actual coding itself, writing to standards and specification, testing and implementation. All these things develop your skills as a programmer and all are important, but are these things enough?

If you immediately answered 'Yes!' to the question above then you are probably not yet quite ready for promotion. On the other hand, if you answered 'Yes, but...', then you are well on the way. Being a good programmer is certainly about being technically competent but there is much more to it than that. Additional skills involve maturity, planning, working successfully in a team, reporting, liaising with users. Sometimes you will not have opportunities to practise all these skills or they simply come with experience. Whatever the reasons, by being aware of such things allows you to work towards them, recognise and acquire them. Success should follow!

When you first begin work you often find yourself being given quite specific and well defined tasks, perhaps to write a reasonably straightforward COBOL program. You complete it to the best of your ability, announce that you have finished and look forward to the next piece of work. You concentrate on working well, completing the task, learning the idiosyncrasies of the compiler and operating system and generally learning your environment. You are working at becoming a good coder. When you have achieved these basic but important objectives there is still much to learn – these are those other skills.

Look at how your more senior colleagues work and your manager. Do they seem to spend a lot of their time discussing things with each other, going to meetings and less time in front of a computer terminal than you? Probably the answer will be 'yes'. They are managing or learning how to manage, whether in terms of you or a project. They are also reporting – reporting progress, work outstanding, work completed etc. at all levels of management and users and clients. They are, in fact, performing many and varied tasks with the objectives of the department, company and their own goals all being taken into consideration – they are trying to do their job better.

Communication

Communication? What do we mean by that? We mean reporting to others, either upwards or downwards in management terms, and either formally or informally, written or verbally. You might be thinking that more junior members of staff have no need to report, they simply do a task and shout when it has been completed. This really should not be the case however.

Managing staff is not easy, it is a task that requires dissemination of information at all levels. You can help your manager by volunteering information to him, keeping him updated and letting him know when you are having problems or are generally alright. Learn to drive your manager by telling him what particular stage of your program you have reached, what you think you might be good at or able to help with. Perhaps you have a skill that your manager was not aware of – make it known.

Much of this reporting can be done informally and often in a matter of minutes. By mentioning that you are at the testing stages of your program you are providing management information, although at a very basic level. You are displaying your ability to provide information, show initiative and be a self starter. Such efforts will be appreciated – chasing people for information can be very boring, chasing them repeatedly does not bode well!

So, even at the most basic level, reporting requirements can easily be fulfilled. Remembering to keep your manager informed does not always come naturally. It is a simple but effective art that needs to be practised. Learn it and apply it.

Perhaps more subtly, such reporting methods act as a way of covering oneself. We all slip-up occasionally and kick o' selves afterwards. By informing people of what you are doing, going to do or have done makes them aware and more importantly gives them the opportunity to raise any objections or queries – it allows you to 'cover yourself'.

Covering yourself is one of the important aspects of management. You should be using your manager in two directions, by him telling you what to do and by you telling him what you are going to do. If you make people aware of your intentions and receive no negative feedback or gain approval then they have taken some of the responsibility for your actions. Although this idea might appear a little strong it is still a valid one. Any manager should be prepared to take reasonable responsibility for the actions of his staff – after all he is paid more than you and that is one of the reasons why!

Verbal reporting is very important, if in doubt about something then mention it! We have only considered verbal reporting so far but there are, of course, more formal methods of verbal reporting. Consider how many you can think of.

Working in a team

One of the aspects of work you will come across sooner or later is that of working in a team. In some ways this can actually appear quite a contradictory concept. On one hand you will possibly be part of a large project team whilst on the other, the role of the programmer is often to work on his own.

Appreciating these two ideas goes a long way to becoming a good team member. Working on one's own can be relatively easy. You only have yourself to consider. You schedule your day and the work within it and concentrate on one main task. When you want help you are likely to ask for it but communication may well remain low. Many programmers work like this and it can have a number of advantages; good productivity, high concentration and personal motivation. In a team/project environment the approach has to be different.

Working in a team can at first seem a very alien experience. Individual efforts are still important but a sense of team cooperation and understanding needs to be nurtured and developed – this will be one of the roles of the team leader.

The team leader can work in one of two main ways. Some like to take a very strong leadership/senior programmer role while others operate a more 'democratic' approach where the work is shared amongst the team members and they become very much in control. The former method often works well with more junior members of staff who are likely to require technical help and direction from above. The latter method can work well for more experienced and mature programmers. It is also a good way of identifying natural leaders or those with reasoned thinking skills. Whichever method you become involved with, identify the system and work within it accordingly.

When you become involved in a team situation you should take advantage of the opportunities it affords. You are more likely to be involved with the business function behind the application. You will need to know more about the programs your colleagues are producing and possibly the way they interface with each other. Deadlines may become more important as certain programs become current on the critical path – the results of your yet unfinished program might be required by another programmer further ahead. Clearly much more day-to-day contact is required.

Finally, working in a team creates a sense of compatriotism and responsibility towards others – knowledge can be exchanged providing an excellent learning opportunity.

The many advantages of working in a team include:

(1) Recognising and using the skills of others.
(2) Improving communication skills.
(3) Less dependence on any one person.
(4) Dissemination of business/technical knowledge.

Working with users

On large project developments there can sometimes be the situation whereby you are producing a product for an unidentified end-user. You probably have a reasonable understanding of the overall application and the users in general but are not talking to any users specifically.

Users can come in a multitude of forms, some will be outside clients, others will reside at another office and others again will be in the same building. Users on-site or in-house provide the best chances to improve the skills required when dealing with such people.

Some users will be friendly and helpful, willing to spend time explaining problems or aspects of their job or business. Others will be just as enthusiastic but more elusive and unable to provide much time. Others again will be rude or unhelpful, perhaps feeling threatened or ill informed. As a programmer it will be part of your job to put such people at ease and act in a friendly but professional manner.

There are probably three basic rules to observe:

(1) Be well prepared
(2) Be friendly
(3) Be professional

If, after following all these rules, you still encounter problems, then there is probably little you can do but to persevere.

As you continue to work in what is often a support environment you will learn much about yourself, gain more confidence and a better understanding of the business. You will learn that what people ask for is not always what they want, that many people still do not understand computers (but why should they?) and often wish to be driven by others i.e. the 'tell me what I can have' stance.

If you get into major problems, again, use your manager – ask his advice and learn from his experience. Also remember that the user will nearly always want to help, because without you their requirements will not be met!

A final word

We have considered a number of different areas, both technical and non-technical, from writing a specification, coding rules through to the importance of time management and communication. All are equally important if you aspire to being a rounded and useful skilled COBOL programmer. Read this book, digest it and apply the ideas in a way that suits you and your working environment.

Remember, you might think you are good, but no-one will know unless you demonstrate the fact. So, remember the five basic rules:

(1) Be a communicator
(2) Drive your manager
(3) Show initiative
(4) Be professional
(5) Keep it simple!

Index

action diagrams, 92
activity diagrams, 86
audit-trail, 50

batch-processing, 50, 54
binary trees, 85
boundary clash, 40
box-and-line diagrams, 13, 61

CAD, 95
Case, 13
chairman, 69
change control, 74
CHAR, 106
charting, 80, 82
checking, 17
COBOL, 13, 33, 93, 99, 110
coding, 73
columns, 100
comments, 73
COMMIT, 110
communication, 153
compiling, 78
CONFIGURATION SECTION, 20
control structures, 28
correspondences, 31, 32, 43
CREATE, 105

data, 11, 23, 30
data analysis, 12
data dictionaries, 12, 96
DATA DIVISION, 20
data models, 85
data structures, 31, 41
database, 53
database administrator, 104
decomposition, 13

DELETE, 109
desk-checking, 17
DFD, 88
diamonds, 10
DML, 100
Do While, 24
documentation, 30, 66, 73, 75

ELSEs, 58
embedded SQL, 115, 141
Enddo, 24
entities, 104
entity-relationship diagrams, 90, 103
ENVIRONMENT DIVISION, 20
estimating, 129

file description, 20
file layouts, 24
FILE-CONTROL, 20
files, 28
flowcharts, 10, 84
fourth-generation, 115

Gantt, 128
garbage-in, 28
GOTOs, 58

header records, 29
help, 47, 48
hierarchy, 13

IDENTIFICATION DIVISION, 56
IFs, 13
implementation, 10
indentation, 110
indexed sequential, 29

INITIALISATION SECTION, 15, 20, 61
input, 4, 12
INSERT, 106
interactive programs, 25, 48, 53, 134

LOCKing, 145
logic design, 11

main, 15, 61
management, 153
many-to-many, 90, 104
mapped, 32
meetings, 69
menus, 46
methodologies, 79
Michael Jackson, 23
minutes, 69
motivation, 15

nesting IFs, 58
normalisation, 101
NULL, 106, 109

objective, 11
on-line, 46, 53
one-to-many, 27, 90
one-to-one, 90
order clash, 39
OUTPUT, 4, 12

planning, 128
primary groups, 30
PROCEDURE DIVISION, 58
program characteristics, 46
program coding, 10
program design, 10, 17, 60, 139
program functions, 34
program maintenance, 72
program specification, 3, 9, 10
program structure, 33
program testing, 10, 60, 66, 121, 140
programming standards, 55
pseudo-code, 15, 20

read, 14
relational databases, 99
Repeat, 13
response times, 49
reviewing, 21
ROLLBACK, 110
rows, 100

screen design, 49
scribe, 69
secondary groups, 30
sections, 17, 151
SELECT, 106, 139
selection, 13, 25
sequence, 25, 36
SQL, 53, 99, 100, 115
structure clash, 39
structure indicators, 28
structured programming, 23, 39, 56
structured walkthroughs, 68, 135
sub-queries, 109
system documentation, 79
system flowchart, 4, 95

table, 100
teams, 153
termination, 15, 61
test data, 64
test harnesses, 66
test scripts, 64, 122
timescales, 129
top-down, 11, 86
trailer records, 29
tree structures, 85
tuples, 100

UPDATE, 109
users, 154

validation, 49

WORKING-STORAGE, 20, 51, 57